ASSET PROTECTION

for

Professionals, Entrepreneurs and Investors

Gary A. Forster

SECOND EDITION

Library of Congress Cataloging-in-Publication Data
has been applied for.

ISBN: 978-0-9882183-1-4 (Hardcover)

Printed in China

Preface

This book provides general insight into the strategies available to protect wealth from creditors. It is not a comprehensive legal treatise, but rather a concise explanation of the more pertinent planning strategies. The book also includes historical perspectives to aid the reader in understanding how various asset protection techniques have developed.

Inside you will find a variety of planning tools potentially suitable to a wide scope of professionals, entrepreneurs and investors. Although the book will aid the reader in understanding asset protection law, it cannot be relied on as legal advice. The strategies contained in this book are not a substitute for a professional analysis of any particular circumstances.

Acknowledgments

Without the help of a few people, the book would never have materialized.

I first need to thank my wife, Lorna, for her tremendous patience and consideration. The writing of the book took twice as long as I had promised. It spanned the pregnancy, birth and two birthdays of our first child. Lorna also had the most insightful comments of anyone who read the book before publication.

My mother, Karen, devoted countless hours to helping me compile and type my initial notes to form the early structure of the book. Her devotion to my fixation on detail was instrumental.

Nancy Rarden's superb typing and formatting saved my sanity and made publication possible.

My research assistants, Adam Russo and Ashley Feasley, found just the right legal support and citations to keep me on the "straight and narrow." I am very grateful for their help.

Thank you all for putting up with me.

Gary A. Forster

TABLE OF CONTENTS

Introduction

Asset protection is a developing body of law which sets the boundaries within which to plan for potential creditor claims. Asset protection planning presents a very enticing proposition: If your lifestyle or profession exposes you to litigation and the law offers protection from potential creditors, why not implement such protections?

Unprotected assets are exposed to creditors. Protection is available from a variety of U.S. and foreign sources. Asset protection law is principally drawn from (i) legislation shielding particular assets and (ii) trust and corporate structures within which to protect otherwise vulnerable assets. Asset protection strategies involve the acquisition of creditor exempt assets and titling unprotected asses in trusts and business entities. Although the federal government, the fifty American states and

1

certain foreign governments have enacted laws protecting assets, the laws vary dramatically. Specific planning options depend on the profession, wealth, lifestyle and domicile of the individual.

Laws governing creditor protection are often vague. Ambiguous legislation leaves interpretation to the courts. Appellate court rulings are binding on lower courts and are known as "case law." Judicial discretion (to determine the precise meaning of a statute) leads to unpredictable rulings and uncertainty in collection law. Therefore, the most protective and judicially accepted statutes should be utilized in asset protection planning.

Fortunately, unreasonable judicial interpretation is relatively uncommon. Given the often fruitless pursuit of suing an insolvent or asset protected defendant, relatively little case law defines the limits of effective asset protection. Although most established exemption statutes and trust law may be relied on, the effectiveness of more recent asset protection strategies is largely untested.

Successful asset protection planning is highly dependent on proper implementation before facing creditor claims. The key to an effective asset protection plan is the planning. Once an event of liability has occurred, or a claim has been lodged, protective strategies become unavailable. Although reactionary offshore transfers move exposed assets beyond the reach of domestic courts, evasive measures tend to infuriate judges and have led to contempt orders and jail time. Avoidance of perceived abuses is as important as implementing legal protections.

Most judges have a limited background in asset protection, trust or corporate law. Judges are typically former prosecutors or litigation attorneys with little or no training in the subtleties of trust or corporate structures. Litigation tends to be factually oriented, decided on the merits of "right and wrong." For this reason, protective planning should reflect good faith intentions to implement unambiguous protections, especially when insulating assets located in the U.S.

Each individual should have a uniquely structured asset protection plan, best suited to his or her particular profession, lifestyle and holdings. For example, owners of an active business should segregate business assets from personal assets. Business operations create liabilities which can become the responsibility of the business owner if the business is not properly organized and operated. One basic aspect of any viable asset protection structure is the restriction of business creditors to business assets (to shield the business owner from personal risk). Correspondingly, business assets should be insulated from the personal debts of the business owner.

Many "experts" believe that asset protection can only be successfully accomplished as a side effect of estate or corporate planning. In other words, planners often take great pains to reflect an estate planning or business purpose as the primary motivation for protective restructuring. This approach has some validity because corporate or estate planning intentions may negate a creditor's claim that assets (used to fund a business or estate plan) were transferred to hinder collection.

3

However, pretending that asset protection is a collateral concern (to pacify a judge later ruling on the structure) may miss the point.

Enforceable protections can be implemented solely to protect assets from creditors. Furthering multiple purposes may be efficient, but priorities should be precisely defined. Attaining one goal could compromise another. For exam₁ le, estate tax planning often involves gifting and transfer strategies that can undermine optimal asset protection planning. If estate planning is the priority, the most effective asset protection tools may not be available.

Although not a condition to creditor protection, addressing beneficial estate planning and corporate strategies may be prudent. Depending on the circumstances, asset protection planning can potentially be accomplished as part of estate or corporate planning. Business structuring, for example, involves limiting the liability of partners, officers and directors.

Much of the value derived from asset protection planning lies in the financial barrier confronted by creditors attempting to collect protected assets. Even modest asset protection planning will arm the debtor with a legal basis to defend collection. Such defenses translate into increased litigation costs for the plaintiff (or the plaintiff's attorney suing to recover a contingency fee). Litigation expense establishes a minimum recovery amount, below which the creditor will lose money by suing. Protective planning inevitably raises the minimum recovery floor.

The justification for asset protection is illustrated by the case evaluation methods of the trial attorney. Trial attorneys (typically practicing personal injury or products liability law) pay the costs of litigation (with the intention of sharing in the judgment collected by the client). Trial attorneys are the street fighters of litigation, seasoned in summing-up a defendant and calculating the risks and rewards of entering the ring. When a trial lawyer is presented with a potentially insolvent, uninsured or asset protected defendant, the pugilist will generally pass on risking the time, energy and money necessary to win a likely uncollectible judgment. Trial lawyers intimately understand that the merits of a lawsuit will not pay the legal fees.

Conversely, the "civil litigator" (also referred to as a "commercial litigator") typically works through a larger firm with corporate, real estate and other types of business attorneys. The business firm usually cannot accommodate the risk of losing the fees and costs associated with a contingency fee arrangement. The commercial litigator must bill the plaintiff by the hour (independent of the financial risks or winnings of the client). The client alone bears the risk of losing the case (or winning an uncollectable judgment). As a result, the relationship between the civil litigator and his client can be quite tense.

In light of the commercial litigator's lack of financial motivation to collect a judgment, commercial disputes are litigated on the merits of the claim (not the likelihood of the defendant to pay a judgment). Commercial cases against defendants armed with a sound asset protection plan are often initiated, but eventually settled (when the plaintiff becomes aware that prompt payment is unlikely).

The following chapters discuss a variety of asset protection planning strategies.

Chapter 1: Our Legal System

"[Common law] stands as a monument slowly raised, like a coral reef, from the minute accretions of past individuals, of whom each built upon the relics which his predecessors left, and in his turn left a foundation upon which his successors might work." – Learned Hand (1922)[1]

1.1 Common Law System

Our "common law" system differs radically from what are known as the "civil law" jurisdictions (found in continental Europe and South America). Civil law

---

[1] Learned Hand, Book Review, 35 Harv. L. Rev. 479 (2922) (reviewing Benjamin N. Cardozo, *The Nature of the Judicial Process*, (1921).

systems are based on a detailed "Napoleonic style" legal code, strictly applied by a fact-finding judge. There are no juries. The U.S. "common law" system relies on trial juries to apply the facts of a case to existing law. Appellate judges interpret statutory law and reshape existing case law through facts presented by new cases. The U.S. inherited the English common law system which reveres as fundamental the right to trial by one's peers.

Legislators often pass ambiguous statutes, leaving the determination of the precise meaning of the law to judges and juries, on a case by case basis. Appellate case law generally governs new cases with similar facts. A new appeal with distinct facts may allow (or even require) the court to create new "case law." Unlike the civil law system, the common law often affords the presiding judge substantial discretion to determine the rights and remedies of the litigants.

The common law system allows for the use of common sense rulings to distinguish the facts of a particular case and to prevent an inappropriate outcome (which is not uncommon in a rigid civil law context). In other words, the common law system promotes the "spirit of the law" rather than simply the "letter of the law." One obvious drawback to the system is, however, the uncertainty created by juries and judicial discretion. Thus, even in seemingly clear cut matters, the litigants cannot determine with certainty how a jury or appellate court will rule.

Judicial discretion has, for example, resulted in a generally unbounded U.S. tort liability system. Potential personal injury claims and monetary recoveries are limited only by the imagination of the plaintiff's attorney. For example, the average size of jury awards for medical malpractice increased 76% from 1996 to 1999.[2] In 2009, the average size of large jury verdicts increased from $112 million to $145 million.[3] A few recent jury awards reflect the random and emotional nature of U.S. tort litigation.

- $370,000,000 dollars for defamation in California, where five former employees of Georges Marciano, Guess jeans co-founder, counter sued Marciano, after Marciano accused the employees of stealing his identity.

- $300,000,000 class action tobacco lawsuit in Florida, where the plaintiffs suffer from permanent emphysema.

- $157,000,000 wrongful death damages from a malfunctioning of a tree stand in Indiana.

- $60,000,000 for medical malpractice for a botched plastic surgery in New York.

---

[2] See Jay Copp, A Profession at Risk, American Association of Neurological Surgeons, Vol. 20, Issue 3 (2001) *available at* http://www.aans.org/Media/Article.aspx?ArticleId=10022

[3] Tony Ogden, The Verdict is in Top 10 Jury Verdicts of 2010, Detroit Legal News, Jan. 21, 2011, *available at* www.legalnews.com/detroit/845937.

- $49,000,000 for brain injuries suffered in a car accident in Illinois.

- $29,600,000 for injuries that the plaintiff received from a train accident in Illinois.

- $2,860,000 for pain from a cup of hot coffee that spilled in the plaintiff's lap in New Mexico.

- $2,300,000 for injuries suffered by a drunk plaintiff who stumbled in front of a subway train in New York.

1.2   Courts of Equity

The early English legal system was rigid and technical due to its reliance on the "writ" pleading system. A writ permitted an Englishman to sue one of the King's subjects under certain limited circumstances. The writ system allowed legal remedies only for specific writs (later known as "causes of action"). If no writ existed for the harm suffered, no recourse was available.[4]   The introduction of new legal remedies through the King's early "law" courts was therefore very difficult. The alternative ecclesiastical courts (with jurisdiction over spiritual and personal matters, such as marriage and divorce) often had no jurisdiction to rule on claims with a remedy at law. If no remedy for an injured party existed in

---

[4] Albert Hutchinson Putney, *Introduction to the Study of Law*, Popular Law Library, 167 (Cree Publishing Co.) (1908).

10

the common law or in the ecclesiastical courts, the injured party had one avenue of recourse: to petition the king or his council for relief. Traditionally, it was the king's chancellor who received these petitions. Over time, the king's chancellor became "custodian of the king's conscience," implementing rules of fairness and justice (rather than legal technicalities), to ensure the injured party some form of redress.[5] The arrangement became known as "courts of equity."

Even after personal matters were secularized and removed from the jurisdiction of the English ecclesiastical courts, the courts of equity remained as a parallel legal institution to the common law courts.[6] The American colonies inherited this legal structure. The U.S. federal government later combined the common law and equity courts, to empower a judge to render judgments based on principles of law or equity, depending on the circumstances of the case. Principles of justice based on equity still operate today. This is especially important in the area of asset protection where equity or "fairness" test the limits of permissible planning. For example, if the debtor is a so-called "bad actor" the court may be tempted to disregard applicable protections as unfair.

---

[5] George Gleason Bogert, Handbook of the Law of Torts, 10 (West Pub. Co., St. Paul) (1921).

[6] A.D.E. Lewis ed. History of English Law, 20 (External Pub., London, 2nd Ed.) (1998).

1.3   Common Law and Asset Protection
       Planning

Considering the judicial discretion (and uncertainty) inherent in our common law system, asset protection techniques should take advantage of established legal protections without raising the specter of abuse. In other words, a plan should clearly comport with existing statutes and case law protections. If challenged, the plan should not afford the presiding judge any ambiguity as to the facts surrounding the implementation of the plan or the legal protections implemented.

An example of a protective structure arising from the common law is the irrevocable trust. Historically, the irrevocable trust is funded by a "grantor" or "settlor" for the benefit of a separate "beneficiary." The grantor has no access to trust assets. The irrevocable trust is a tried and true mechanism for the protection of trust assets. Laws protecting assets controlled by a "trustee," for a beneficiary, may be traced back hundreds of years and have been codified by all fifty states.

Trusts naming the settlor as a beneficiary are called "self-settled" trusts and do not traditionally protect trust assets from creditors of the settlor. Twelve U.S. states have, however, introduced statutory "asset protection trusts" which allow a grantor to fund a trust for the grantor's own benefit. These states are Alaska, Colorado, Delaware, Hawaii, Missouri, Nevada, New Hampshire, Rhode Island, South Dakota, Tennessee, Utah and

Wyoming.[7] Such trusts stray from classic common law parameters by allowing the grantor to fund his own protective trust. Protective "self-settled" trusts are an example of recent protections not yet validated by the courts. Although protective "self-settled" trusts have historically only been available offshore, since 1997 these twelve U.S. states have enacted legislation protecting such trusts. In light of the historical prohibition of protecting trust assets available to the grantor, the enforceability of such protections remains unclear and subject to judicial revision. Caution should therefore be taken before implementing untested protections such as domestic self-settled trusts.

Federal and state "exemption" statutes independently protect certain assets. Such statutes require no special trust or ownership structure. The more precise the statutory protection, the lower the likelihood of judicial "legislation." For example, if a state protects the cash value of life insurance held by its residents, it may not be clear that the protection extends to "variable universal" life insurance. In a case where a judge feels it unfair to shield an asset from a legitimate creditor, even the slightest ambiguity in protective language could be construed against the debtor.

The most effective planning limits judicial discretion by implementing historically accepted trust and

---

[7] Charles D. Fox IV, Hawaii Enacts Domestic Asset Protection Trust Litigation and Reinstates Separate State Estate Tax, McGuire Woods Newsletter, 3 August 2010, *available at* www.mondaq.com/unitestates/article.asp?articleid=106992

business entities, along with precise statutory exemptions. The more deeply rooted the common law method of protection, the less likely the judge will tamper with the plan. The clearer the statutory language protecting a particular asset, the less room for judicial interpretation contrary to protective goals. The good faith of the debtor and the corresponding clear purpose or public policy behind a protective statute (such as creditor exemptions for homestead and retirement assets) will also diminish the chances of judicial intervention.

Chapter 2: The History of Asset Protection

"The trust is a complex legal organism that survives on private property.   Its earlier forms predate even the Norman conquest.   The trust . . . is the product of centuries of evolution.   [It is] an 'institute' of great elasticity and generality; as elastic, as general as a contract."- Charles Rounds (1999)[8]

2.1   English Trust Law

The practice of asset protection planning likely began as a reaction to the common law of England. In the middle ages, the feudal system imposed onerous financial

---

[8] Charles E. Rounds, Jr., *Loring – A Trustee's Handbook* 3-4 (New York: Aspen Publishing, Inc. 1999).

15

burdens on real estate owners, entitling the lord of the land to "relief." Relief typically consisted of payments by the "feoffor," or owner of the property. Payments were due upon the occurrence of certain events, such as the passage of the property to an heir, the marriage of a daughter, the knighting of the eldest son or the holding of a "tenant" for ransom.

To avoid paying relief, English property owners would "enfeoff," or transfer legal title to, a "foeffee to uses" (later known as a "trustee"). The foeffee was bound by agreement to direct profits and sales proceeds to a "cestui que use" (later known as a "beneficiary").[9] This 11th century maneuver allowed the owner to avoid the financial burdens of legal title. Vesting legal title in a trustee also took advantage of the absence of any creditor rights to trust property. Neither the settlor, trustee or beneficiary had rights to trust assets that could benefit their creditors. An Englishman could place assets with a trusted friend or relative "in trust" for his children. The trustee was bound by the terms of the trust and could not personally benefit from or expose trust assets.

Trusts were also used to: (i) defeat the collection of taxes, (ii) prevent the government from taking assets of an individual who committed treason, and (iii) defeat claims of tenants against landlords. Additional benefits of shifting ownership to a trustee are the avoidance of public disclosure and cost associated with transferring real estate

---

[9] George G. Bogert, et al., The Law of Trusts and Trustees § 2 (3d ed. 2007).

from one generation to the next. Trust property is protected and the identity of the beneficiary kept secret.

"Uses" (the early name for trusts) became so popular in medieval England that, by the time of Henry V (1413-1422), they were the predominant form of land ownership. Thus spawned the fifteenth century origins of modern asset protection planning. Medieval trusts were so effective that no legal means initially existed to reach assets transferred by criminals or debtors to a trustee. Property subject to forfeiture or foreclosure could not be reached by the creditor (or victim) once transferred into trust. To obviate the injustice created by the right to avoid a creditor, the predecessor of the present day Fraudulent Transfer Act was enacted. Such law is discussed in Chapter 6.

English history often causes Americans to equate modern asset protection with trust law. Americans continue the English tradition by utilizing trusts to safely pass wealth from one generation to the next. The trust is the living precursor of modern asset protection.

2.2   Bankruptcy

2.2.1   Bankruptcy Cases as a Resource

American case law is established by appeals court precedent. State and federal appeals courts therefore define the limits of enforceable asset protection techniques. Creditors, however, rarely invest in an appeal (potentially creating new case law), without the prospect of a large payday. For this reason, indigent or asset protected debtors are typically not worth pursuing. As a result, collection litigation has spawned relatively few appellate "case law" rulings. The boundaries of permissible asset protection have consequently developed very slowly in the state courts. In the absence of state case law, we must look to federal bankruptcy cases to interpret creditor rights.

Bankruptcy litigation is all about the legal determination of a debtor's right to retain valuable assets. Although bankruptcy generally involves a petition to discharge indebtedness (owed by an insolvent debtor), the debtor must (in a Chapter 7 bankruptcy) surrender certain assets to creditors. Bankruptcy judges are consistently forced to rule on whether valuable assets held by the debtor are available to creditors. The legal theories and reasoning of bankruptcy courts often address the precise asset protection issues involved in civil collection matters. Federal bankruptcy cases therefore provide valuable insight into how state civil courts will handle collection actions.

2.2.2   Bankruptcy Law in General

The federal bankruptcy process generally provides a means of discharging indebtedness owed by an insolvent debtor. The assets of the debtor become the property of the "bankruptcy estate," paid to creditors, based on rules of preference. The debtor seeks the discharge of all debt and exposure of as few assets as possible to creditor claims. Assets protected by federal or state law are exempt from collection in bankruptcy. However, if the state of the debtor's residence "opts out" of federal exemptions, only state (and not the federal) exemptions apply.[10]

Generally three types of bankruptcies are available to individuals and businesses: Chapter 7, Chapter 11, and Chapter 13. Chapter 7 contemplates a "snapshot" liquidation on the date of filing. Non-exempt assets are compiled for collection by unsecured creditors (whose debts are discharged). Exempt and protected assets are retained by the debtor, and money earned after filing bankruptcy (i.e., after the snapshot) is not available to creditors. The debtor is generally discharged from almost all unsecured indebtedness within ninety days of filing and provided a "fresh start."

As an alternative, Chapter 13 affords individual debtors the ability to establish a repayment plan. Only individuals with unsecured debts of less than $360,475 and secured (collateralized) debts of less than $1,081,400 are eligible for Chapter 13 bankruptcy. If a debtor is able to repay the restructured debt, the debtor may keep his or her assets.

Chapter 11 is available only to businesses and individuals with significant assets and debt exceeding the

---

[10] Opt-out states include Alabama, Arizona, California, Colorado, Delaware, Florida, Georgia, Idaho, Illinois, Indiana, Iowa, Kansas, Louisiana, Maine, Maryland, Mississippi, Missouri, Montana, Nebraska, Nevada, New York, North Carolina, North Dakota, Ohio, Oklahoma, Oregon, South Dakota, Tennessee, Utah, Virginia, West Virginia and Wyoming.

Chapter 13 limits. Under Chapter 11, the debtor remains "in possession" of its assets and proposes a debt payment plan. Under certain circumstances, the debtor may force the creditors to accept (or "cram down") the payment plan. If the debtor complies with the payment plan, the debtor retains its assets.

State statutory creditor exemptions (of particular assets) are available only to residents of protective states. A substantial presence, or (depending on the state) just the intent to live in the state, is required to qualify for such exemptions. To prevent state residency "shopping" by debtors contemplating bankruptcy, the 2005 Bankruptcy Act requires the debtor to establish state domicile for two years prior to filing. Only after the two year residency period may a bankrupt debtor exclude assets exempted by such state. If the debtor was not domiciled in the state offering the exemption for such required two year period, then the state where the debtor was domiciled during the 180 day period preceding the two year period will be considered the state of domicile. To take advantage of a state homestead creditor exemption, the bankruptcy debtor must reside in the applicable state for 1,215 days.[11]

Unfortunately, these burdensome residency requirements apply to all bankruptcy debtors, even those residing in "opt-out" states.[12] The debtor in the "opt-out" state who fails the two year residency test must resort to protections offered by his prior state of residence or the

---

[11] *In re Kaplan*, 331 B. R. 483, 487 (Bankr. S.D. Fl. 2005).
[12] *Id.*

limited federal exemptions. Bankruptcy can be an obstacle to asset protection planning by limiting use of state creditor protections.

Filing voluntary bankruptcy potentially exposes otherwise exempt assets to creditors. Even if voluntary bankruptcy is avoided, creditors may be able to force a debtor into involuntary bankruptcy (to reach otherwise exempt assets). If the debtor has fewer than twelve creditors, a single creditor may force the debtor into bankruptcy. If the debtor has more than twelve creditors, three creditors may force the debtor into involuntary bankruptcy. Ironically, bankruptcy can be used as a creditor remedy to reach assets otherwise unavailable in state court.

Chapter 3: Modern Trust Law

"It is a fundamental policy of our law that the owner of an estate in fee simple may alienate or subject it to payment of his debts at any and all times. Any attempt to evade this right... must be declared void. No legal estate in fee, in tail, or for years can be restrained absolutely. The only possible exception to this is ... a spendthrift trust." – *Arthur W. Blakemore (1914)*[13]

    Trusts are the historical foundation of modern asset protection planning. Although trusts may take a variety of forms, only three parties are necessary to form a Trust: a "settlor", a "trustee" and a "beneficiary." The

---

[13] Arthur W. Blakemore, Modern American Law: *Law of Real Property*, Vol. 5, § 134 (Blackstone Inst. London) (1914).

settlor (also known as "grantor") forms and funds the trust. The trustee is named to manage the trust. The beneficiary is the recipient of trust assets (distributed by the trustee, as directed in the trust). Each of the three positions may consist of one or several people. Two types of trusts are typically utilized in domestic asset protection planning: (i) the modern spendthrift trust and (ii) the domestic asset protection trust. (See Section 2.1 for a discussion on the origins of trusts.)

3.1   The Modern Spendthrift Trust

The practice of appointing a third party to control assets for a beneficiary has evolved into a legal arrangement known as the "spendthrift" trust. A spendthrift trust prevents the beneficiary from selling or assigning his interest in trust income or principal. Spendthrift trust assets may be distributed to a trust beneficiary, but only pursuant to the terms of the trust. The beneficiary holds no legal title to trust assets. The beneficiary has no right to manage, spend, transfer or encumber trust assets. The beneficiary's interest in trust assets or distributions may not therefore be transferred (either voluntarily (to a purchaser) or involuntarily (to a creditor)).

The creditor protection associated with the (non-assignable) spendthrift trust is typically augmented by leaving absolute discretion regarding trust distributions with the trustee. Creditors of a trust beneficiary may only reach assets available to the beneficiary. Vesting control over trust distributions in the trustee avoids the transfer of any property rights to the beneficiary and leaves creditors of the beneficiary with nothing to pursue. Only trust distributions (whether mandated by the trust or made at the trustee's discretion) may be reached by creditors of the beneficiary. The separation of legal ownership and control from the benefit of trust assets creates the protection associated with discretionary spendthrift trusts. This is the oldest and most respected form of asset protection.

In addition to creditor protection, the spendthrift trust allows for the passage of assets to beneficiaries who are either incapable or too young to prudently manage trust property. The trust may, however, be used to create the so called "trust fund baby" (i.e. beneficiaries not financially accountable for their behavior). Spendthrift trusts may even support malicious offspring, whose trust income cannot be reached by creditors, even through litigation. The enforceability of the spendthrift trust concept was validated by the U.S. Supreme Court in an 1875 case, *Nicholas v. Eaton*.[14] Despite the controversy associated with creating "trust fund babies," the arrangement has been codified by all U.S. states.[15]

Public policy has led to a few exceptions to spendthrift creditor protection in all but a few jurisdictions. Most state trust statutes expose trust assets to the extent necessary to avoid offending generally accepted social and moral values. For example, in all states, apart from Alaska

---

[14] *Nichols v. Eaton et al.*, 91 U.S. 716 (1875).
[15] *See Scheffel v. Krueger*, 146 N.H. 669, 671-2 (2001), interpreting New Hampshire's spendthrift provision, N.H. Rev. Stat. Ann. § 564-23 (2001).

and Nevada, the spouse or child of a trust beneficiary may reach trust assets under certain circumstances (generally involving familial support). Also, providers of certain necessary goods and services (required to maintain a reasonable standard of living) may generally enforce a claim against a spendthrift trust. Depending on the state, other exceptions to spendthrift creditor protection may include debts of the beneficiary to personal injury creditors,[16] creditors who provided services to protect the beneficiary's interest in the trust[17] or the United States government.[18] As discussed in Section 6.1, the foreign debtor haven trust statutes do not include any such exceptions.

The creditor protection afforded domestic trusts depends on the grantor's irrevocable gift to the trust. Contrary to the irrevocable trust, the so called "revocable trust" provides no creditor protection because it may be amended or revoked by the grantor at any time. The grantor typically serves as the sole beneficiary of the "trust." No additional trustee or beneficiary is necessary during the grantor's life. The revocable trust does not (during the grantor's life) shift control or benefit of assets away from the grantor. Assets titled in a revocable trust therefore remain available to creditors of the grantor.

Interestingly, Oklahoma protects trust assets from creditors of the grantor, even if the trust is revocable. Oklahoma, however, protects only trust assets benefitting

---

[16] *In re the Estate of Gist*, 763 N. W. 2d 561, 566-68 (2009).
[17] *See e.g.* La. Rev. Stat. Ann. § RS 9: 2005(2) (2004).
[18] *See e.g.* Fl. Stat. § 736.0503(e) (2011).

the grantor's family (not the grantor) as "qualified beneficiaries."[19] Also, the likelihood of enforcement of such protections by a court outside Oklahoma is speculative.

The revocable trust functions in a way similar to a last will and testament, to establish the grantor's disposition of assets at death. Although much like a will, assets may be titled during the grantor's lifetime in the revocable trust, to avoid probate at death. Upon the death of the grantor, the revocable trust may fund one or several irrevocable (protective) "testamentary" trusts, for the benefit of the grantor's spouse, minor children, etc.

Unfortunately, revocable trusts are often implemented by estate planners without integrating applicable protections. For instance, titling a principle residence in a revocable trust may cause the loss of statutory homestead creditor protection in some states. Also, revocable trusts cannot be used by a married couple to jointly hold assets by the entireties (a protective form of ownership discussed at Section 4.8).[20]

---

[19] Oklahoma's "Family Wealth Preservation Act, 31 Okla. Stat Ann §§ 19-17 (2004); Okla. Stat. § 31-11 (2005).

[20] See Del. C. § 3334, protecting property in a Delaware revocable trust to the extent contributed by husband and wife as tenants by the entirety ("TBE") (by retaining TBE protection from trust creditors during the lifetime of both spouses, leaving creditors the sole remedy of directing the trustee to transfer the property to both spouses TBE).

3.2   Domestic Asset Protection Trusts

The protective benefits of domestic trusts have historically applied only to trust beneficiaries other than the grantor. The classic spendthrift trust conditions asset protection on the grantor contributing to a trust for the benefit of someone else. This has been true in England since the 1400s and, until recently, respected by all U.S. states.[21] Trusts which make assets available to the grantor or name the grantor as beneficiary are called "self-settled" trusts. Self-settled trusts do not traditionally protect trust assets from the grantor's creditors.

Grantors seeking trust protection and the continued benefit of trust assets have been forced offshore. Since the advent of the foreign asset protection trust in 1984[22], several offshore jurisdictions have passed legislation allowing the grantor to benefit from trust assets not available to creditors. Foreign trusts also facilitate the placement of assets outside the jurisdiction of U.S. courts. The often prohibitive cost of forming and maintaining an offshore trust and potentially onerous tax treatment have, however, generally precluded all but the very wealthy from utilizing such a "self-settled" foreign trust.

In an effort to attract filing fees and deposits (otherwise sent abroad), several U.S. states have adopted "self-settled" trust legislation similar to that offered by

---

[21] George G. Bogert, et al., The Law of Trusts and Trustees, § 2 at 18 (3d ed. 2007).

[22] Cook Islands International Trusts Act of 1984, reprinted on 2 December 1999, *available at* http://www.trustnet.com.hk

foreign debtor havens. The combined allure of spendthrift protection and of the right to form a trust benefiting oneself has led to legislation establishing domestic asset protection trusts ("DAPTs") in thirteen states. The domestic asset protection trust provides reduced costs and tax reporting, the comfort of working within the U.S. banking and legal structure, and avoidance of the scrutiny associated with foreign entities.

In 1997, Alaska established the first domestic "self-settled" trust and Delaware soon followed. The other states (listed in Chart 3.2) are more recent to the arena. Such states allow a settlor to fund a "spendthrift" trust for his or her own benefit. The trust protects assets from creditors of the settlor by placing them within the control of a third party trustee. Modern offshore and domestic self-settled trust are therefore known as "asset protection trusts." All DAPTs must be irrevocable and must place substantial discretion in a trustee who is not the settlor.

DAPT statutes (unlike offshore trust laws) generally require that (i) the trust be irrevocable and spendthrift (i.e., not assignable by the grantor/beneficiary), (ii) the grantor not act as trustee, (iii) the trustee reside in the particular state of organization and (iv) at least some trust assets be held in the same state (generally in a bank or brokerage account). Several states restrict the settlor's ability to terminate the trust. DAPTs are also subject to the applicable fraudulent transfer laws. (See Chapter 5 for a discussion on fraudulent transfer laws.)

Although all DAPTs permit a grantor to fund the trust for the grantor's own benefit, the legislation differs from state to state regarding the treatment of the grantor's creditors. For instance, all DAPT jurisdictions except Nevada allow access to trust assets by certain preferred creditors.[23] Such creditors of the grantor include current and prior spouses, children and lenders. Nevada provides no preference to any class of creditor.[24] DAPT assets are also subject to collection by the federal government, because federal collection rights trump any conflicting state statute. Chart 3.2 reflects some of the statutory characteristics and requirements of self-settled trusts in each domestic jurisdiction. All other states reject the notion of protecting assets placed in trust for the grantor.

Although untested by the courts, the general academic consensus is that residents of a DAPT state will likely find the DAPT protective of trust assets. Courts outside such state may feel no compulsion to abide by protections in conflict with local trust law.

The first U.S. judgment regarding a DAPT will be afforded "full faith and credit"[25] by all U.S. courts. A ruling confirming the viability of DAPTs will become the subject of constitutional reciprocity and enforceable in all fifty states. Although the U.S. Constitution does not require each state to apply the domestic trust laws of

---

[23] *See e.g.*, Del. Cod Tit. 12, Ch. 35 §3573, *available at* http://delcode.delaware.gov/title12/c035/sc06/index.shtml; Ak. Stat. § 34.40.110 (2009).

[24] Nev. Rev. Stat. Tit. 13, Ch. 163 §5559.

[25] U.S. Const. art. IV. § 1.

Chart 3.2

Domestic Self-Settled Asset Protection Trusts
Selected Statutory Characteristics

State	Right of Settlor To Distributions	Some or All Trust Assets Must Be Held in Trust State	In-State Trustee Required	Powers Settlor May Retain
Alaska	Trustee discretion plus fixed percentage of trust value ("total return trust") and interest in tax-driven trusts (CRT, QPRT, GRAT)	Suggested	Suggested	Veto distributions; appointment of protector
Colorado	Statute silent	Statute silent	Statute silent	Statute silent
Delaware	Trustee discretion plus current income, 5% total return trust; reimbursement for income taxes attributable to payments of estate costs and interest in tax-driven trusts	Required	Required	Veto distributions; replace trustee
Hawaii	Trustee discretion plus 5% of value of trust assets and (if written into the trust) rights to trust income distributions for income taxes and estate costs and taxes; CRT, GRAT, QPRT	Required	Required	Veto distribution; replace trustee; appoint protector; general power of appointment
Missouri	Trustee discretion (trust must also include as beneficiary in addition to settlor)	Statute silent	Required (principal place of business or administration in or trustee is a resident of Missouri)	None
Nevada	Trustee discretion; trust income, CRT, GRAT and QPRT	Not required	Required if settlor domiciled outside Nevada	Veto distributions; remove and replace trustees; direct trust investments
New Hampshire	Trustee discretion plus current income; 5% total return trust; estate costs; income tax attributable to trust	Required	Required	Veto distributions; replace trustee with unrelated party; serve as trust advisor
Rhode Island	Settlor discretion plus current income; 5% of total return trust; income tax attributable to trust and QPRT	Required	Required	Veto distributions
South Dakota	Trustee discretion plus current income, 5% total return trust; tax-driven trusts	Required	Required	Veto distributions; replace trustee with unrelated party
Tennessee	Trustee discretion plus current income, 5% total return trust; CRT and QPRT	Required	Required	Veto distributions; replace trustee with unrelated party; serve as investment advisor
Utah	Trustee discretion plus interest in CRT	Required	Required	Veto distributions; appoint non-subordinate protector
Virginia	Trustee discretion to income and principal; CRT	Required	Required	Remove and replace trustee
Wyoming	Trustee discretion plus current income; 5% total return trust; CRT and QPRT	Required	Required	Veto distributions; add or remove trustee, protector or trust advisor; serve as investment advisor; power of appointment

another state, future case law upholding any self-settled trust legislation will likely bring the domestic asset protection trust into the mainstream. If upheld by the courts, the U.S. self-settled trust will serve as a reliable domestic alternative to the foreign asset protection trust (without the expense, inconvenience and skepticism associated with foreign trusts). However, until validated by a U.S. court, U.S. trusts benefitting the grantor cannot be relied on to insulate trust assets.

The advantage of "full faith and credit" could also prove to be a weakness. A savvy creditor may successfully establish collection litigation in a creditor friendly state. To establish a jurisdictional tie to the creditor friendly state, the creditor must prove that the debtor or trustee is a resident of, doing business, or maintaining assets in the creditor friendly state. An institutional trustee (with offices across the country) could conceivably subject the trust to several jurisdictions. If an adverse jurisdiction is established, creditor claims that public policy requires the court to apply local trust law (contrary to the terms of the trust) should be anticipated. If a judgment establishes that trust assets are available to creditors, the judgment may be registered and collected in any state with trust assets (even in the state which wrote the law governing the self-settled trust[26]).

A collection ruling in a creditor friendly state which weakens or invalidates a particular "self-settled" trust may potentially erode the strength of the particular

---

[26] *Franchise Tax of California v. Hyatt*, 538 U.S. 488 (2003).

(and potentially all) domestic asset protection trust legislation. (See also page 104 regarding challenges to trust law governing real estate.) DAPTs are untested by the courts and should (until validated) be used with caution.

Overall, offshore asset protection trusts allow for more flexible planning than domestic trusts. While domestic self-settled trusts typically require local investment and a local trustee, foreign havens do not. Additionally, unlike domestic self-settled trusts, foreign asset protection trusts are not invalidated by empowering the grantor with the right to act as trustee, to remove trust assets or terminate the trust.

Foreign trusts also more comprehensively preclude creditor attack. While domestic self-settled trusts typically grant certain creditors access to trust assets, offshore havens exclude even familial obligations. The offshore havens permit limited fraudulent transfer claims and do not recognize U.S. laws or judgments. Domestic trusts are also subject to the claims of the U.S. Government. IRS and Bankruptcy collection rights therefore defeat any inconsistent state exemption statutes. Foreign trusts operate outside the U.S. legal structure. (See Section 6.1.2 for a more detailed discussion of offshore trust benefits.)

Chapter 4: Exempt Assets

"Theoretically, you could shelter the Taj Mahal in [Florida] and no one could do anything about it." Justice A. Jay Cristol (1993)[27]

All fifty states and the federal government have delineated certain assets as exempt from creditors. No protective structure is necessary to insulate such assets. Apart from a very narrow list of creditors (generally

---

[27] Larry Rohter, *Rich Debtors Finding Shelter Under a Populist Florida Law*, N.Y. Times, July 25, 1993 *available at* http://www.nytimes.com/1993/07/25/US/rich-debtors-finding-shelter-under-a-populist-florida-law.html, quoting Judge A. Jay Cristol, Chief Judge Emeritus, U.S. Bankruptcy Court, Southern District of Florida.

limited to state and federal governments, marital claimants and lien holders), exempt assets are untouchable.

Depending on the state, protected assets may include the value of the home, farm, life insurance, annuities and retirement accounts. Federal law also protects certain retirement and other assets from attachment by creditors (even in bankruptcy). Given that exemption statutes insulate particular assets, judicial activism (based on the court's "interpretation" of a statute) is rare. Although this book discusses some of the more interesting state and federal exemptions, the discussion is not exhaustive. Individualized planning by a local specialist is essential.

Investment in exempt assets should be methodical. Planning typically involves the conversion of exposed liquid assets (such as cash and securities) to less liquid assets (such as insurance products). For this reason, exempt assets should be thought of as both unavailable to creditors and not essential for short-term needs. Some liquid funds should always be kept available (even if exposed), to the extent necessary to pay living expenses or the cost of defending a lawsuit or collection action. Without liquidity, the debtor/defendant may be forced to "open the vault" (i.e. breach his or her planning structure) to cover litigation expenses.

4.1   Residency Requirements

Individual residents (or, if applicable, "domiciliaries") of states protecting particular assets may take advantage of statutory exemptions. While most states require a "substantial presence" in the state, others require only "domicile" (the intent to live in the state permanently). Owning a residence in a state is not the same as being a resident of that state. The determination of residency is factually sensitive. A debtor may be domiciled in one state while residing in a different state.[28] Some states (for example, Florida) allow the filing of a "declaration of domicile" to help prove the intent to live in the jurisdiction permanently. The declaration is considered a factor in determining an individual's intent to establish permanent residency in Florida.[29]

4.2 Homestead

4.2.1 Homestead in General

One of the most popular state exemptions is the "homestead exemption." Although 47 of the 50 states offer some protection of the principal residence, the benefits vary from state to state. Unfortunately, only six states offer an unlimited homestead exemption. All other states restrict the amount of homestead value protected from creditors. If a homeowner in a state with a limited exemption becomes subject to a judgment creditor, the protected value of the home is limited to the state's exemption amount. The creditor may foreclose the home and retain all sales proceeds beyond the exemption

---

[28] *See e.g.*, Fl. Stat. §§ 222.17(2), 196.012(17)(18), 196.015, regarding declaration of domicile and defining and determining permanent residence in Florida.

[29] Fl. Stat. § 196.015.

Asset Protection

amount. Chart 4.2.1 lists the various state homestead exemptions.

Chart 4.2.1   **State Homestead Exemptions**

State	Single Exemption Amount	Married Exemption	Acreage Limit	Size Limit by Location
Alabama	$5,000	$10,000	Yes	No
Alaska	$54,000	$54,000	No	No
Arizona	$150,000	$150,000	No	No
Arkansas	$2,500	$2,500	Yes	Yes
California	$50,000	$75,000	No	No
Colorado	$45,000	$45,000	No	No
Connecticut	$75,000	$75,000	No	No
Delaware	None	None		
District of Columbia	None	None		
Florida	Unlimited	Unlimited	Yes	Yes
Georgia	$5,000	$5,000	No	No
Hawaii	$20,000	$30,000	Yes	No
Idaho	$50,000	$50,000	No	No
Illinois	$7,500	$15,000	No	No
Indiana	$7,500	$15,000	No	No
Iowa	Unlimited	Unlimited	Yes	Yes
Kansas	Unlimited	Unlimited	Yes	Yes
Kentucky	$5,000	$10,000	No	No
Louisiana	$25,000	$25,000	Yes	Yes
Maine	$12,500	$25,000	No	No
Maryland	$6,000	$12,000	No	No
Massachusetts	$500,000	$500,000	No	No
Michigan	$3,500	$3,500	Yes	Yes
Minnesota	$200,000	$200,000	Yes	Yes
Mississippi	$75,000	$75,000	Yes	No
Missouri	$15,000	$15,000	No	No
Montana	$100,000	$100,000	No	No
Nebraska	$12,500	$12,500	Yes	Yes
Nevada	$200,000	$200,000	No	No
New Hampshire	$100,000	$200,000	No	No
New Jersey	None	None		

38

State	Single Exemption Amount	Married Exemption	Acreage Limit	Size Limit by Location
New Mexico	$30,000	$60,000	No	No
New York	$10,000	$10,000	No	No
North Carolina	$10,000	$20,000	No	No
North Dakota	$80,000	$80,000	No	No
Ohio	$5,000	$10,000	No	No
Oklahoma	Unlimited	Unlimited	Yes	Yes
Oregon	$25,000	$33,000	Yes	Yes
Pennsylvania	None	None		
Rhode Island	None	None		
South Carolina	$5,000	$10,000	No	No
South Dakota	Unlimited	Unlimited	Yes	Yes
Tennessee	$5,000	$7,500	No	No
Texas	Unlimited	Unlimited	Yes	Yes
Utah	$10,000	$20,000	No	No
Vermont	$75,000	$75,000	No	No
Virginia	$5,000	$5,000	No	No
Washington	$40,000	$40,000	No	No
West Virginia	$5,000	$5,000	No	No
Wisconsin	$40,000	$40,000	No	No
Wyoming	$10,000	$20,000	No	No

The homestead exemption applies only to property held by one or more individuals. In several states, the exemption may be lost by titling the residence in a revocable living trust. Transfer to one or more revocable trusts also typically precludes joint titling by husband and wife, as tenants by the entirety (discussed at Section 4.8). Despite the common advice of estate planners to transfer the home to a revocable trust (to avoid probate), such titling may expose the home to creditors in some states. The same is true regarding transfers to the so called "land trust," generally used to hide the identity of property owners. Contrary to the sales pitches, beneficiaries are easily discovered in litigation and the revocable land trust provides no asset protection.

If the debtor is not a resident of Florida, Iowa, Kansas, Oklahoma, South Dakota, or Texas, the homestead exemption is limited (subjecting the home to attachment and sale). Any existing mortgages and liens are first paid. Sales proceeds exceeding the mortgage are paid to the debtor, but only to the extent of the homestead exemption. Any remaining equity is available to the creditor. Sheltered proceeds from the sale of homestead property must typically be reinvested in an exempt asset to remain protected.

If the exemption from creditors is limited, the property may likely be protected by placing it in an LLC or protective partnership (discussed at Section 7.2), domestic asset protection trust (discussed at Section 3.2), and/or titling the home (or protective entity) as tenants by the entirety with rights of survivorship (discussed at Section 4.8). The protections derived from transfer of the home to a protective entity, must be weighed against the costs. Potential disadvantages of transfer are (i) higher property tax rates, (ii) loss of federal tax benefits (i.e., the tax deduction for interest payments and exemption of capital gains tax on sale ($250,000 for a single owner and $500,000 for a married couple), (iii) LLC/partnership or trust start-up and maintenance costs, (iv) acceleration of any existing mortgage with a "due on sale" clause and (iv) loss of title insurance.

Although the entire homestead value is protected in a small minority of states, the unlimited protection is conditioned upon certain qualifications. Such conditions include: the size of the property (within a limited acreage), the state's minimum residency requirements and proper titling and use of the property (as a principle residence). Homes exceeding the applicable acreage limitation, for example, may be attached and sold by creditors.

The Supremacy Clause of the U.S. Constitution permits the federal government to ignore conflicting state law.[30] Federal law subjects all residences to federal tax liens and certain domestic support obligations. Any homestead may therefore be seized by the IRS.

Local construction liens on homestead property will also generally defeat the homestead protection. Additionally, a mortgage holder in the homestead property may obviously foreclose a defaulted loan secured by the property.

Florida offers the broadest homestead protection. Florida's constitutional homestead protection is illustrative of the respect afforded statutory exemptions by the judiciary.

4.2.2   Florida's Homestead Exemption

The Florida state Constitution provides:

---

[30] U.S. Const. art. VI, cl. 2.

There shall be exempt from forced sale . . . or . . . lien . . . except for the payment of taxes and . . . obligations contracted for the purchase, improvement or repair. . . the following property . . . : a homestead, if located outside a municipality, to the extent of one hundred sixty acres or, if located within a municipality, to the extent of one-half acre . . . .[31]

Although Florida's homestead protection is clear, the proverbial "devil" is in the details. For example, Florida allows the foreclosure of homestead property based on tax liabilities or construction liens on the property. Any judgment creditor may also force the sale of a residence located inside a Florida municipality if (i) the size of homestead property exceeds one-half acre and (ii) the property may not be subdivided.

The famous *Havoco* case reflects the influence of legislative clarity and public policy regarding Florida's homestead exemption.[32] In *Havoco*, Mr. Hill, a bankruptcy debtor, invested unprotected funds in a Florida home. The transfer was intended to avoid the claims of an existing creditor and thus violated the Florida Fraudulent Transfer Act (discussed at Chapter 5 below). The Florida Supreme Court, however, ruled that the home remained exempt from creditors (despite the fraudulent transfer).

In 1990, Mr. Hill, a long-time Tennessee resident, invested in a Florida house eleven days after a jury verdict

---

[31] Fl. Const. art. X, §4.

[32] *Havoco of Am. Ltd., v. Hill*, 790 So.2d 1010 (Fla. 2001).

subjected him to a $15,000,000 judgment. Mr. Hill purchased a $650,000 home in Florida and claimed that he intended to reside permanently in the state. He then filed for bankruptcy to discharge the judgment against him. The Florida Supreme Court ruled that Florida's fraudulent transfer laws (permitting the attachment of funds transferred to avoid a creditor) do not apply in the context of the homestead exemption. Furthermore, the Court suggested that equity may be sheltered in both a purchased home or by paying an existing mortgage encumbering a Florida homestead.

Florida's constitutional exemption therefore shelters assets otherwise available to existing or anticipated creditors. Although such "fraudulent transfers" are otherwise reversed in favor of the creditor, the language and public policy behind Florida's homestead exemption have apparently eliminated the ability of even a judgment creditor to reach equity in a Florida homestead.[33] Only misappropriated funds invested directly in a Florida primary residence may be reached. The Florida Supreme Court has, in effect, invited debtors in other states to purchase homestead property in Florida, even if their intention is to avoid the legitimate claims of creditors. No other state protects assets fraudulently transferred. Florida's homestead protection arguably offers the strongest creditor protection in the U.S.

---

[33] *Id.*

4.2.3 Bankruptcy and *Havoco*

Until the 2005 Bankruptcy Act, funds subject to a fraudulent transfer claim could be freely sheltered in a Florida residence. This is no longer the case in bankruptcy. Also, paying a home mortgage[34] with exposed cash (to avoid loss of the cash to a bankruptcy creditor) may now preclude bankruptcy discharge of indebtedness. In a bankruptcy case where the debtor paid a home mortgage with money otherwise available to the bankruptcy trustee, the bankruptcy court denied discharge of indebtedness and imposed a lien on the home. The ruling allows the bankruptcy trustee to sell the home for the benefit of creditors.[35]

Pursuant to the 2005 Bankruptcy Act, only $125,000 (adjusted annually for inflation) of homestead equity may be sheltered under a state exemption during the 1,215 days prior to bankruptcy. In other words, the debtor must own the home longer than 1,215 days before filing bankruptcy to avoid the $125,000 limitation on sheltered homestead equity. Due to the 2005 Act, a debtor such as Mr. Hill may no longer transfer non-exempt property (such as cash) to his new Florida homestead and proceed to file bankruptcy. Instead, the revised rule requires him to own the property for 1,215 days prior to filing. The $125,000 limitation is subject to certain restrictions and does not apply in certain circumstances. For instance, protected value may be transferred from a principal residence

---

[34] *In re. Chauncey 2005 WL 2456223* (S.D. Fla. 2005), *aff'd in part, rev'd in part*, 454 F.3d 1292, 1295 (11th Cir. 2006).
[35] *Id.*

(acquired prior to the 1,215 day period) to a new residence without restarting the 1,215 day limitation, but only if the new home is in the same state. As noted in Section 2.2.2, the $125,000 bankruptcy limitation applies even to residents of states which have "opted out" of the federal bankruptcy exemptions.[36]

Consider the practical impact of filing bankruptcy in Florida. If the defendant in a civil case shelters cash by paying down his mortgage, the plaintiff (even if successful in obtaining a judgment) may not reach the cash. If the invested funds cannot be traced to money wrongfully obtained, the creditor must attempt to force the debtor into involuntary bankruptcy. If successful, and if the debtor has not owned the home for 1,215 days, the unlimited homestead protection is lost. Involuntary bankruptcy proceedings may therefore expose all but $125,000 of the debtor's homestead equity. Bankruptcy similarly exposes other exempt assets if the debtor was not domiciled in the protective state for two years prior to the bankruptcy filing.

4.3   Retirement Plan Accounts

4.3.1   ERISA

In 1974, Congress enacted the Employment Retirement Income Security Act ("ERISA") to address several high profile pension collapses of the 1960's and

---

[36] *In re Kaplan*, 331 B.R. 483, 487, (Bankr. S.D. FL 2005).

70's.[37]   Congress established ERISA to encourage employers to fund retirement plans by providing an income tax deduction for employer contributions. ERISA qualification requires federal compliance through various funding, accounting and legal formalities.

To qualify for ERISA, retirement plan assets must be held in an irrevocable spendthrift trust. The trust must prohibit the transfer of plan assets by participants. The transfer restriction insulates retirement plan assets from creditors of participants by placing plan assets in the exclusive control of a trustee. The Bankruptcy Code also excludes from collection assets subject to such a transfer restriction. The U.S. Supreme Court confirmed such protection in 1992.[38]   The public policy behind the Supreme Court's interpretation of ERISA is the encouragement of national savings by placing pension assets beyond the reach of creditors. In so ruling, the Supreme Court stated that: "Our holding gives full ... effect to ERISA's goal of protecting pension benefits. [The] goal [is] ensuring that if a worker has been promised a defined pension benefit upon retirement . . . that . . . he actually will receive it."[39]

Generally, employer sponsored plans are protected by ERISA and independent employee maintained plans (such as IRAs and SEPs) are not. The popular 401(k) employer based savings plan, for example, is an ERISA

---

[37] *See* Employee Retirement Income Security Act of 1974 "ERISA" (Pub. L. 93-406, 88 Stat. 829), Sept. 2, 1974.

[38] *Patterson v. Shumate*, 504 US 753, 757-59 (1992).

[39] *Id.* at 765.

(protected) plan. Also included among ERISA plans are profit sharing plans, money purchase plans, target benefit plans and defined benefit plans. IRAs, simplified employee pension accounts (SEPs), stock options and certain tax qualified plans (generally benefitting business owners) do not qualify for ERISA protection. Although a plan may qualify the participant to defer income tax on contributions, it may not provide federal asset protection.

Plan assets will lose ERISA protection if "rolled over" into an employee's independent IRA or distributed (unless protected by state law). If the state where the owner resides does not protect a particular non-ERISA retirement plan, plan assets are exposed to creditors. The following is a list of ERISA qualified plans:

- Defined Benefit Plans
  ◦ Traditional Pension
  ◦ Cash Balance
  ◦ Keogh

- Defined Contribution Plans
  ◦ 401(k)
  ◦ 403(b)
  ◦ Keogh
  ◦ Employee Stock Ownership
  ◦ Profit-Sharing
  ◦ Money Purchase
  ◦ Target Benefit

4.3.2 Bankruptcy and the IRS

The 2005 Bankruptcy Act protects tax qualified retirement plan assets. Under the Act, a bankruptcy debtor may exempt retirement funds held in a plan formed under Internal Revenue Code §401 (such as the "401(k) plan), §403, §414, §457, or §501(a).[40] The Bankruptcy Act also amended the Bankruptcy Code to protect IRAs (up to $1,000,000, excluding the SEP or simple retirement account).[41] The limit applies without regard to rollover contributions. The $1,000,000 limit may, however, be increased if required in the "interests of justice."[42]

If the Bankruptcy Act fails to exempt assets in a particular plan, the debtor may rely on any applicable state law exemptions.[43] In states that offer no protection, plan assets are subject to bankruptcy creditors. Non-qualified plan assets unprotected by state law should (to the extent permissible) be held in a protective entity (such as a domestic or offshore trust, limited partnership or LLC). Note that a protective entity may not be used to hold an IRA account (but an entity may be a named beneficiary).

ERISA protections do not shield plan assets from the spouse of the participant or the IRS.[44] Nevertheless, the IRS has relaxed its collection position on ERISA assets

---

[40] 11 U.S.C. §§ 522(b)(3)(C), (4)(A).
[41] P.L. 109-8. *See* IRS Private Letter Ruling "P.L.R." 109-8 § 522(a).
[42] *Id.*
[43] 11 U.S.C. § 522(d)(10)(E).
[44] *U.S. v. Sawaf*, 74 F.3d 119, 123 (6th Cir. 1996).

held by a bankrupt taxpayer.[45] The IRS no longer attaches pension plan assets excluded from the bankruptcy estate.[46] Outside bankruptcy, IRS seizure of qualified plan assets remains an exposure. Note that no state taxing authority may reach qualified retirement assets. This is because federal ERISA "preempts" (trumps) any conflicting state tax law.

4.3.3 Non-ERISA Retirement Plans

Although non-ERISA retirement plans (for business owners) do not qualify for federal creditor protection, various states, including Florida, New York, Oregon and Iowa, provide creditor protection for several "non-qualified" plans. For example, New York broadly exempts from creditors "payment under a stock bonus, pension, profit-sharing, annuity, or similar plan or contract on account of illness, disability, death, age, or length of service."[47]

Florida arguably offers the greatest expansion of ERISA protections. Florida protects tax exempt retirement plan assets from creditors of the owner, beneficiary or participant.[48] For example, the Florida Statutes protect certain non-qualified pension plans, profit sharing and stock bonus plans as well as IRAs. Florida also exempts

---

[45] 11 U.S.C. § 506(a).

[46] *See* IRS Office of Chief Counsel Notice, CC-2004-033, September 09, 2004, *available at* http://www.irs.gov/pub/irs-ccdm/cc-2004-033.pdf

[47] *Matter of Carmichael*, 100 F.3d 375 (5th Cir. 1996).

[48] Fl. Stat. § 222.21(2)(a).

assets held in certain retirement plans for county officers, teachers, fire fighters, state employees and police officers.[49] One court ruled that Florida further protects distributions from tax deferred plans without a dollar limitation and imposes only very liberal restrictions on the use of protected funds.[50]

The following states exempt IRA assets without limitation of value: Alabama, Alaska, Arizona, Colorado, Connecticut, Delaware, Florida, Hawaii, Illinois, Iowa, Indiana, Kansas, Kentucky, Louisiana, Michigan, Mississippi, New Hampshire, New Jersey, New Mexico, New York, North Carolina, Oklahoma, Oregon, Pennsylvania, Rhode Island, Tennessee, Texas, Utah, Vermont, Washington and Wyoming.

Several less protective states, such as Arkansas, Indiana, Kansas, Minnesota, Nevada, North Dakota, South Dakota, and Virginia, impose various dollar limitations and restrictions on (i) how retirement funds must be utilized, and (ii) whether cash distributions from exempt plans retain their protected status.[51] Several states, such as Rhode Island, Utah, and Hawaii preclude protection of contributions to non-qualified plans made within a certain number of days prior to the filing of bankruptcy.

---

[49] *See, e.g.,* Fl. Stat. §§ 122.15 (county officers, employees), 175.241 (for firefighters), 185.25 (for police officers), 121.131 (for state officers, employees), and 238.15 (for teachers).

[50] *In re Ladd*, 258 B.R. 824 (Bankr. N.D. Fl. 2001).

[51] *See e.g.* Va. Code § 34-34(A).

The limited state protections offered by California, Georgia, Maine, Massachusetts, Missouri, Nebraska, Ohio, South Carolina, West Virginia and Wisconsin are generally contingent on retirement funds being "reasonably necessary" for the support of the debtor and the debtor's dependents.[52] The 2005 Bankruptcy Act follows a similar family support standard.[53]

Factors indicating necessity may include:
- the debtor's particular living expenses,
- the needs of the debtor's dependents,
- the debtor's income, training and debt,
- the age and health of the debtor and the debtor's dependents,
- the debtor's other assets, and whether such assets are protected and/or liquid,
- the special needs of the debtor and the debtor's dependents, and
- the debtor's ongoing financial obligations, such as alimony or support payments.[54]

In light of potentially expansive state protections, qualification under ERISA may not be essential to protect plan assets. If state statutory protections are available,

---

[52] See 11 U.S.C. § 522(d)(10)(E), Fl. Stat. § 222.201, incorporating 11 U.S.C. § 522(d)(1)(E) by reference.

[53] 11 U.S.C. § 522(d)(10)(E) provides an exemption for "[t]he debtor's right to receive ... a payment under stock bonus, pension, profit sharing, annuity, or similar plan or contract on account of illness, disability, death, age, or length of service, to the extent reasonably necessary for the support of the debtor and any dependent of the debtor .... "

[54] In re Vickers, 954 F.2d 1426, 1427, fn. 3 (8th Cir. 1992).

great care should be taken to satisfy applicable statutory requirements. The exposure of mandatory retirement distributions and the solvency of plan participants should also be considered, due to the potential exposure of non-qualified plan assets to bankruptcy.

4.4   Exemption of Wages

All 50 states provide some type of creditor exemption for income earned as wages. "Wages" are salary or hourly pay. Wages do not include profits distributions. Wage planning involves segregating wages from other funds, to preserve their character as salary, compensation, etc. Employment is generally necessary to create fixed and periodic compensation. To establish wage protection, self-employed individuals should act as their own employee. This is accomplished by making the owner a W2 employee of the business.

Similar to the homestead exemption, the wage exemption varies dramatically from state to state. Several states, such as Delaware and Alabama, protect only a portion of wages. Other states, such as South Carolina and Texas, exempt all wages from judgment creditors of the earner.

Florida's treatment of wages is instructive. Florida protects all qualified wages (referred to as "disposable earnings") from "garnishment." Wage garnishment is a creditor action to force an employer (or someone else holding earnings) to pay the creditor directly. The creditor garnishes the funds before they reach the debtor for consumption. Florida exempts all wages earned by the "head of a family" and a limited amount of "disposable earnings" earned by anyone other than the head of a family. Such disposable amount equates to the exemption under the Federal Consumer Credit Protection Act (discussed below).[55]

Florida law recognizes the importance of segregating protected wages from unprotected funds. As wages are often not immediately consumed, Florida shelters wages for six months after bank deposit.[56] Wages deposited by the head of household are therefore creditor exempt for six months. A condition to the extended wage protection in Florida is the consistent deposit of wages into a segregated bank account (to make wages easily identifiable).[57]

The Federal government also protects wages. The Consumer Credit Protection Act[58] limits the amount of wages subject to garnishment to the lesser of: (i) 25% of disposable net earnings, or (ii) weekly earnings exceeding 30 times the Federal minimum hourly wage per week.[59] The Act does, however, permit attachment of wages by certain creditors (including child support claims, Chapter 13 bankruptcy orders and state and federal tax levies).[60] Interestingly, the Act does not protect wages deposited

---

[55] Fl. Stat. § 222.11(2)(c).

[56] Fl. Stat. § 222.11.

[57] Fl. Stat. § 222.11(3).

[58] 15 U.S.C. § 1601, *et. seq.*

[59] 15 U.S.C. § 1673(a).

[60] 5 U.S.C. § 1673(b).

into a bank (i.e., not consumed), even if segregated and identifiable.[61] Only certain state law protects wage deposits.

4.5   Life Insurance

In its most basic form, life insurance establishes the insurer's contractual obligation to provide money to a beneficiary upon the death of the insured. Insurance policies involve three parties. The "owner" of the policy pays the premiums and controls the policy. The policy is underwritten based on the life of the "insured." The "beneficiary" receives the insurance proceeds (upon the death of the insured). Life insurance therefore shifts the risk of financial loss arising from premature death from the beneficiary (typically a dependent of the insured) to the insurer.

Families risk financial ruin if family income is lost due to the death of the breadwinner. Life insurance provides replacement income and liquidity for payment of estate and other taxes, probate costs and additional expenses. Without liquidity, families may be forced to sell basic necessities to cover living expenses and the costs resulting from the insured's death. Business partners can also employ life insurance to fund the "buy-out" of equity held by a deceased partner.

---

[61] *Dunlop. v. First Nat'l Bank of Az.*, 399 F. Supp. 855, 856-57 (D. Ariz. 1975).

Life insurance proceeds are, however, included in the taxable estate of the owner (even if a beneficiary designation was made). This may be remedied by having the policy owned by an irrevocable trust. With the help of a professional, life insurance can be sheltered and utilized to preserve assets for generations. However, poor life insurance planning may result in estate tax on the insurance itself.

4.5.1   Types of Life Insurance

Two basic forms of life insurance have developed over the last several decades: term life insurance and whole life insurance. Whole life policies are known as "permanent" insurance because they do not expire. Whole life is funded during the life of the insured, accumulates a cash surrender value, and pays upon the death of the insured. Permanent insurance is a dependable source of liquidity for estates potentially burdened with federal estate tax and other costs. In addition to death benefits, contributions to a whole life policy which exceed insurance costs accumulate over time. The policy accumulates an intrinsic "cash surrender value" which may be borrowed, withdrawn or used to cover the cost of the underlying life insurance.

Term life policies, on the other hand, have no intrinsic cash value and insure only premature death within a specific coverage period. Unlike permanent insurance, term insurance expires at the end of the coverage period. Term insurance payments are typically fixed (or "level") and calculated to provide the same or decreasing insurance coverage during the term of the policy. Term insurance is a less expensive means of shifting the risk of unforeseen death (as opposed to creating cash value or guaranteed liquidity at the end of a long life). Term policies are designed to create the liquidity necessary to replace family income or a key employee who dies unexpectedly.

The two basic forms of life insurance have developed into an array of life insurance products. Policies are now available with the combined characteristics of both term and permanent life insurance. Several such additional types of policies include the following:

- Accidental Death Insurance — Term coverage which pays out upon the death of the insured, if the death results from an accident. Travel and flight insurance are examples of this type of policy.

- "Second-to-Die" or Joint life insurance — Term or permanent coverage that insures the lives of two or more people and pays upon the death of the last insured to die. The "second-to-die" feature has become popular between husband and wife, in light of the unlimited estate tax marital deduction which postpones estate tax until the death of the surviving spouse. The extended term generally reduces premium costs below the typical "first-to-die" policy.

- Universal Life Insurance — Lifetime coverage that allows broader investment of cash value. Although the policy does not expire, insurance costs are typically deducted from the value of investments held within the policy. Successful investment will cover annual insurance premiums and provide a return on investment. However, insufficient investment returns could necessitate further contribution, to cover insurance costs.

- Variable Life Insurance — A form of universal life insurance (often referred to as "variable universal life insurance") which allows the owner to choose the type of investments held within the policy (typically a variety of mutual funds). Similar to universal life, investment losses can create exposure to premium deficiencies (if investments fail to cover insurance costs).

4.5.2   Life Insurance as a Protected Asset

Several states and the U.S. government support life insurance planning by exempting cash values and proceeds from creditor claims. The debtor may act as one or all of the three basic policy participants (i.e., owner, insured and/or beneficiary). Typically, the protected interest is the beneficial interest (supporting family income and liquidity).

Life Insurance and Bankruptcy

The Federal Bankruptcy Code contains a limited ($10,775) creditor exemption for the cash surrender value of life insurance owned by the debtor.[62] To qualify, the insured must either be the debtor or a dependent of the debtor. The cash value exemption in bankruptcy applies without inquiry, as long as either the debtor or the debtor's spouse is the insured.[63] The debtor's spouse does not need to prove dependency to be considered a dependent of the debtor.

The Bankruptcy Code exempts all life insurance proceeds from collection in bankruptcy, but only to the extent "reasonably necessary" to support the debtor and any dependent.[64] The protection reflects Congress' intent to shelter only necessary family death benefits. Any applicable state exemption should be utilized in bankruptcy to protect cash values and proceeds from policies implemented for tax and estate planning purposes.

State Protections of Life Insurance

State statutory protections vary regarding (i) the amount of cash value and/or proceeds protected and (ii) the types of creditors (i.e., of the insured, owner or beneficiary) exempted.

---

[62] 11 U.S.C. § 522(d)(8) states it is $10,775. *See also* 11 U.S.C. §§ 522(a)(1);(d)(8)(2007).

[63] *Id.*

[64] 11 U.S.C. § 522(d)(11)(C) 609, 611; 11 U.S.C. 522(d)11(C) (2007).

Cash Value

Although most states do not protect the cash surrender value of whole life insurance, states like New York exempt cash values from creditors of the policy owner. Florida exempts the entire cash surrender value, but only from creditors of the insured. Cash values held by a Florida owner other than the insured are exposed. For example, in Florida, the cash value of a policy owned by the spouse or business associate of the insured is not protected from creditors of the policy owner. Hawaii exempts the entire cash value, provided that the policy is payable at maturity to the family or dependent of the insured.[65] The bankruptcy court will respect an unlimited state exemption of cash values.[66]

Life Insurance Proceeds

States such as Alaska and Alabama protect payments made upon the death of the insured (without limit) if the beneficiary is the insured's spouse or dependent.[67] Other states, such as Vermont and Washington, also provide unlimited creditor protection to

---

[65] Ha. Rev. Stat. § 431:1-232(a).

[66] *In re White*, 185 F. Supp. 609 (D.C. W. Va. 1960).

[67] *See Al. Stat. Sec. 27-14-29(b), which provides in part: "If a policy of life insurance ... is effected by any person on the life of another in favor of the person effecting the same or except in cases of transfer with intent to defraud creditors ... the beneficiary shall be entitled to the proceeds ... [i]f the person effecting such insurance or the assignee of such insurance is the wife of the insured, she shall also be entitled to the proceeds .... Al. Stat. Sec. 27-14-29(b)(1971).*

the beneficiary, but only if the beneficiary is not the insured's estate.

Florida[68], New York[69], Hawaii[70] and Louisiana[71] exempt the entire amount of life insurance proceeds. Florida excludes only creditors of the insured (not creditors of the beneficiary or owner, if different from the insured). For example, a child beneficiary in Florida exposes life insurance proceeds to creditors of the child. Children beneficiaries living in Florida should typically benefit from life insurance proceeds only through a spendthrift trust. This may be accomplished by creating a trust to own and act as beneficiary of the policy. This is also a common estate planning strategy, to keep the policy proceeds out of the owner's taxable estate. Upon the death of the insured parent, the trust receives all insurance proceeds directly, outside the reach of the beneficiary's creditors. If a parent intends to maintain lifetime ownership of the policy (as opposed to contributing the policy to a lifetime trust) or if no tax planning is necessary, a spendthrift trust benefitting the child may be named beneficiary upon the death of the owner/insured.

New York excludes only creditors of policy owners from insurance proceeds, depending on a myriad of circumstances.[72] Hawaii also exempts creditors of the

---

[68] Fl. Stat. §§ 222.13-14; 222.13(1); 14 (2011).

[69] *See* L. of N.Y. § 3212(4)(b)(1).

[70] Ha. Rev. Stat. § 431:10-232 (1987).

[71] La. Rev. Stat. Ann. § 22:647 (2006) La. R.S. §§ 22:912(1), (2) (2009).

[72] *See* L. of N.Y. § 3212(b)(2), (b)(3), (b)(4)(A) and (B).

policy owner, with the restriction that proceeds be payable to family or dependents of the insured. Louisiana exempts all proceeds, provided that the policy was not issued within nine months of filing bankruptcy.[73] Unlike Florida, insurance proceeds paid to a surviving child (beneficiary/owner) in New York, Hawaii or Louisiana cannot be reached by the child's creditors. Such creditor protections do not, however, typically apply to dependent and spousal support obligations or alimony claims.

Naming one's "estate" as beneficiary will expose all proceeds to the owner/insured's creditors. If the insured is the named beneficiary, insurance proceeds are paid to the insured's probate estate (subjecting all proceeds to the deceased's creditors). In light of the variations in state law, thorough planning must include consideration of the state of residence and all possible exposures of the insured, owner and beneficiary. Chart 4.5.2 reflects a variety of state life insurance exemptions.

4.5.3   Foreign Life Insurance

Several foreign nations shelter unlimited insurance cash values and death benefits underwritten within their borders. Such jurisdictions include Switzerland and Lichtenstein. Foreign insurance policies are governed by foreign law which generally inhibits U.S. judicial interference. Pursuant to such policies, foreign law applies to all collection and fraudulent transfer claims associated with the policy. Also, cash values and securities held in a

---

[73] La. Rev. Stat. Ann. § 22:647 (2006); La. R.S. § 22:912(2)(2009).

Asset Protection

Chart 4.5.2

Selected State Life Insurance Exemptions

State	Exempt Cash Value	Exempt Proceeds
Alabama	If payable to the debtor's spouse and/or the debtor's children of the marriage	
Arkansas	Exempt if payable to beneficiary other than insured	
California	Yes, but aggregate loan values exempt only up to $9,700 ($19,400 for spouses)	To extent reasonably necessary for support of debtor, spouse, and dependents
Colorado	Cash surrender value exempt up to $50,000	Yes
Connecticut	Dividends, interest, and loan value exempt up to $4,000	If payable to beneficiary other than the insured
Delaware	Proceeds fully exempt if payable to beneficiary other than insured	
Florida	Cash surrender value of policy issued upon the life of a Florida resident fully exempt	From creditors of insured, if paid to beneficiary other than insured or insured's estate
Georgia	Cash value issued upon the life of a Georgia resident exempt	Yes, if paid to beneficiary other than insured or insured's estate, unless the policy says otherwise
Hawaii	If payable to spouse, child, parent, or dependent	
Idaho	If payable to beneficiary other than insured	
Illinois	If payable to spouse, children, parent, or dependents	
Indiana	If payable to spouse, children, dependent, or creditor	
Iowa	If beneficiary is spouse, child, or dependent	
Kansas	If payable to beneficiary other than insured's estate	
Kentucky	Proceeds fully exempt if payable to beneficiary other than insured	
Louisiana	Exempt	
Maine	Policy value fully exempt; accrued interest dividends, and loan value exempt up to $4,000	Exempt if payable to beneficiary other than insured
Maryland	If beneficiary is spouse, child, or dependent	If beneficiary is spouse, child, or dependent; also, money payable from insurance on account of the death of any person is exempt from execution, or a judgment
Massachusetts	If payable to beneficiary other than insured	
Michigan	If payable to spouse or children	
Minnesota	Accrued dividends, interest, or loan values, up to $8,400, if owned by debtor and insured is debtor or dependent	Against creditors of person effecting policy, if payable to beneficiary other than individual effecting policy.
Mississippi	If not payable to insured's estate	If not payable to insured's estate, up to $50,000
Missouri	Yes, with restrictions in bankruptcy	No
Montana	If payable to beneficiary other than insured	
Nebraska	Up to $100,000, if payable to beneficiary other than insured's estate	If payable to beneficiary other than insured's estate
Nevada	Benefits attributed up to up to $15,000 in annual premiums of a proportionate benefit if premiums exceed $15,000. Exempts proceeds against creditors of insured and all beneficiaries, determined when proceeds are made available. The application of the monetary limit to the general exemption is unclear.	

State	Exempt Cash Value	Exempt Proceeds
New Hampshire	None	From creditors of person who established policy if beneficiary is someone other than person who established policy
New Jersey	Cash surrender value and dividends fully exempt	If payable to beneficiary other than insured
New Mexico	Possibly for New Mexico residents	Possibly exempt but subject to taxes and garnishment
New York	Yes, if payable to third-party beneficiary	
North Carolina	During insured's life if policy is for the sole use and benefit of insured's spouse or children	If payable to beneficiary other than insured
North Dakota	For North Dakota residents, if payable to spouse, children, or dependents	To the extent reasonably necessary for the support of the debtor and dependents
Ohio	Cash value if payable to spouse, children, dependents, charity, creditor, but loan values not exempt	If payable to spouse, children, dependents, charity, or creditor
Oklahoma	All benefits exempt	
Oregon	If payable to beneficiary other than estate of insured	If payable to beneficiary other than person effecting insurance
Pennsylvania	Up to $100 per month if insured is beneficiary of policy	If payable to spouse, children or dependents
Rhode Island	If payable to beneficiary other than insured	
South Carolina	From creditors of the insured, if beneficiaries are spouse, children, or dependents	
Tennessee	If payable to spouse, children, or dependents; if paid to an intestate insured's estate for spouse or children, or; if paid to a testate insured's estate and not pledged to the debts of the insured	
Texas	All benefits	
Utah	Unmatured life insurance contract owned by debtor	If paid or payable to spouse or children
Vermont	Yes	If payable to beneficiary other than insured
Virginia	Yes, but cash and loan values not exempt if insured may change the beneficiary	If payable to beneficiary other than insured
Washington	Yes, unless insured may access cash value	If payable to beneficiary other than insured
West Virginia	If payable to beneficiary other than insured	
Wisconsin	Yes, but accrued dividends, interest or loan value of unmatured policy limited to $150,000	If payable to beneficiary other than insured's estate
Wyoming	If payable to beneficiary other than insured	
Washington, D.C.	For D.C. residents and persons earning major portion of livelihood in D.C.; For D.C. non-residents, cash surrender value is exempt if payable to beneficiary other than insured	If payable to beneficiary other than insured

foreign policy are often located in the debtor haven, making attachment by U.S. creditors difficult. In any case, if you live in a state that does not adequately shelter life insurance, several offshore jurisdictions offer a more protective alternative.

4.6   Annuities

4.6.1   Domestic Annuities

Almost all states protect annuities and annuity proceeds to varying degrees. An annuity is a contract where an individual, known as the "annuitant," purchases a stream of payments for a fixed period or over a lifetime.[74] The IRS generally requires (i) that annuity payments be made at regular intervals over a period exceeding one year and (ii) that payment amounts or the annuity period be determinable when the annuity begins.[75] Depending on the terms of the contract, payments may continue during the lives of several beneficiaries and/or end with a lump sum payment.   Payments can be "variable" (based on a stock index or investment assets), variable but hedged (to provide a minimum payment) or fixed.   Annuities may also include a "refund feature," to ensure recovery of the initial investment.

---

[74] N.C. Gen. Stat. §§ 1C-1601, 58-58-95, 58-58-115; N.C. Gen. Stat. § 1C-1601(a)(6); N.C. Const. art. X, §5 (1977) are statute and state constitutional provisions that exempt life insurance proceeds from creditors (as applied to spouse and children).

[75] I.S.R. Pub. 939, General Rule for Pensions and Annuities, rev'd April 2003, *available at* http://www.irs/gov/pub/irs-pdf/p939.pdf.

The cost of the annuity is generally derived from (i) the size of each payment, (ii) the number of payments (based, for example, on the annuitant's expected lifespan), and (iii) additional factors (such as interest rate expectations and options like a lump sum death payment). The price of lifetime annuity payments is based on factors similar to those used to underwrite the cost of life insurance. If payments end upon a premature death (unlike life insurance), the issuer gains a windfall. If, however, the annuitant lives longer than expected, he or she will receive payments exceeding the underwritten cost of the annuity.

The risk analysis of underwriting an annuity is the opposite of life insurance. The annuitant pays a one time lump sum (as opposed to periodic lifetime insurance premiums). The longer the annuitant lives, the more payments the annuitant receives. With life insurance, the longer the insured pays premiums, the more the insurer earns on the policy.

Annuities purchased from an insurance company are known as commercial annuities. An annuity may also be established between family members. Typically, a senior family member ("grantor") gifts assets to younger members of the family, subject to the grantor's right to the income produced by such assets. Such "private" annuities involve gifts to trusts, family entities, etc., by a grantor who "retains" (from the assets gifted) an annuity for a fixed period. The annuity retained reduces the value of the taxable gift. If the grantor survives the annuity term, the assets contributed are removed from the grantor's taxable estate. A popular form of such an arrangement is the grantor retained annuity trust, or "GRAT." A similar strategy is to contribute a residence to a trust and "retain" use of the property for a fixed term (to discount the value of the taxable gift). If the grantor survives the retained term, the home is removed from the grantor's taxable estate. The maneuver is called a qualified personal residence trust ("QPRT").

Another tax strategy is to fund a charitable remainder trust ("CRT") through a tax deductible charitable gift. The grantor gives assets to a trust benefitting a charity, but retains lifetime income (somewhat like an annuity) from the assets donated. The irrevocable trust provides asset protection (insulating the source of the income). Upon the grantor's death, the trust assets are distributed to the charity. Ideally, the value of the tax deduction and the avoidance of capital gains and estate tax on the assets donated will be greater than the value of the gift.

Annuities may be structured to pay a fixed periodic amount or a variable payment. "Variable" annuities pay based on the success of underlying investments funding the annuity contract. As with variable life insurance, the amount of each periodic disbursement to the owner depends on the fluctuating market price of the investments held in the annuity. When payments fluctuate based on investment values, the owner of the annuity assumes the risk (and reaps the benefits) of the fluctuating payment. Conversely, when the classic fixed payment annuity is elected, the insurer assumes the investment risk.

Typically, states that protect life insurance also exempt annuities from creditors. Florida, for example, exempts annuity proceeds without a dollar limitation.[76] In general, Florida courts have supported a broad interpretation of the term "annuity."[77] For example, a Florida appellate court protected a structured settlement received for a wrongful death claim as an "annuity."[78] A bankruptcy court in Florida also ruled that the debtor's transfer of $350,000 to a trust for his children, nieces and nephews, in exchange for $3,000 per month, established an annuity protected by Florida Statute §222.14. The court ruled that the retained payment stream was exempt from creditors, in spite of the debtor having filed bankruptcy thirteen months after establishing the annuity contract. The court based its ruling on the finding that "(1) ...the statutory exemption is not restricted to annuities provided by completely unrelated public entities, and (2) ...[there was] no intent to defraud creditors in the debtor's conversion of his non-exempt assets to exempt assets through the establishment of this annuity contract."[79]

Other courts have, however, warned that an annuity must be more than simply a sale for installment payments.[80] The rulings require, for example, the intent of

---

[76] Fl. Stat. § 222.14 (2011).

[77] *See e.g.* State, Dept. of Ins. v. Great Northern Insured Annuity Corp., 667 So. 2d 796, 799 (1st DCA 1995) (discussing the history of annuities in Florida).

[78] *In re McCollam*, 612 So. 2d 572, 574 (1993).

[79] *In re Mart*, 88 B.R. 436, 438 (Bankr. S.D. Fl. 1988); Cf. *In re Gefen*, 35 B.R. 368 (Bankr. S.D. Fl. 1984).

[80] *In re Conner*, 172 B.R. 119 121 (Bankr. M.D. Fl. 1994).

the parties create an annuity contract.[81] The mere existence of scheduled payments over time is not sufficient.

Several states, such as Delaware[82] and Pennsylvania[83] only partially exempt annuity payments from creditors.[84] The exemptions are modest, to protect only a basic standard of living. Ohio protects payments only if the name 1 beneficiary is the debtor's spouse, children or dependents.[85] All states protect annuities to some extent. Some of the more substantial state creditor exemptions are described in Chart 4.6.1.

The Bankruptcy Code protects only annuity payments made due to "illness, disability, death, age, or length of service." Payments must also be "reasonably necessary" for the support of the debtor . and any dependents. The federal rule therefore protects only payments triggered by an immediate need. Missouri employs the federal bankruptcy standard[86] and New York protects only the reasonable requirements of the debtor and dependent family.[87] Support requirements of a debtor

---

[81] *In re Solomon*, 95 F.3d 1076 1078 (11th Cir. 1996).

[82] De. Code Ann. Tit. 18 § 2727(a)(2)(2011).

[83] 42 Pa. Cons. Stat. Ann. § 8124(c)(3)(2011).

[84] 42 Pa. Cons. Stat. Ann. § 8124(c)(3)(2011)(exception of annuity payments of $100 per month); De. Cod Ann. Tit. 18 § 2728(a)(2)(2011)(exemption of annuity payments of $350 per month).

[85] Oh. Rev. Code Ann. § 3911.10.

[86] Mo. Ann. Stat. § 513.430(10(e).

[87] L. of N.Y. § 3212(d)(2).

Chart 4.6.1

Selected State Annuity Exemptions

State	Exemption limited to certain beneficiaries	Financial Limitation	Retirement Annuities Only
Alaska		$13,000 for accrued dividends & loan values	
Arizona	Debtor, debtor's surviving spouse, child, parent, brother or sister, or dependent family member as a beneficiary	Must have been owned by the debtor for two years	
Colorado			
Connecticut			X
Florida	Must be issued on the lives of Florida residents		
Georgia	Must be issued to Georgia residents		
Hawaii	Proceeds and cash value exempt if payable to spouse, child, or other dependent		
Illinois	Proceeds and cash value exempt if payable to spouse, child, parent, or other dependent		
Indiana			
Iowa	Issued on the life of a resident of Iowa		
Kansas	Government employees		X
Louisiana			
Maryland	Proceeds payable to spouse, child, or dependent relative		
Massachusetts			
Michigan	Proceeds are exempt from creditor of the person effecting the policy when policy is effected in favor of another individual		
Minnesota	Proceeds are exempt from creditors of the person effecting the policy when policy is effected in favor of another individual		
Mississippi		Generally no exemption for private annuities	X
Missouri	To extent reasonably necessary for support of debtor or the debtor's dependents		X
Nebraska	Proceeds, cash values, and benefits accrued are exempt from claims of creditors of annuitant if payable to a different person and exempt from claims of creditors of the beneficiary if related to annuitant by blood or marriage	Up to $100,000 accrued proceeds, cash values, or benefits	
New Hampshire			X

Asset Protection

State		
New Mexico	Must be issued on the life of a New Mexico resident but may be subject to tax liens and garnishment	
New York	Some exposure to judicial discretion is statute	X
North Carolina		X
North Dakota	To extent reasonably necessary for support of debtor or the debtor's dependents	Exempt up to $100,000 per policy with an aggregate limit of $200,000
Ohio	Contract and proceeds exempt from creditors of annuitant if payable to spouse, children, or dependents of insured, certain charities or any creditor	
Oklahoma		
Rhode Island		X
South Carolina		
Tennessee	Amounts payable to spouse, children or dependent relatives of the insured	
Texas		X
Utah		X
Virginia		
Washington	Up to $2,500 per month	
West Virginia		X
Wisconsin		X
Washington, D.C.	D.C. residents and persons earning major portion of livelihood in D.C.	

and dependents are obviously difficult to anticipate as part of a creditor protection plan.

4.6.2   Foreign Annuities

Many foreign countries protect the value of annuities and annuity payments from creditors. Switzerland, for example, exempts annuities payable to the policy owner's spouse and/or dependents. A Swiss annuity may (under the governing Swiss law) be reached only by means of a fraudulent conveyance action if (i) the policy owner filed for Swiss bankruptcy within a year of making or changing the beneficiary designation on the annuity or (ii) the beneficiary designation was made within five years of a creditor action, with the intent to defraud creditors (and the beneficiaries knew of such intent).[88]

To promote the Swiss financial system, Swiss courts may hesitate to allow attachment of a Swiss annuity funded by fraudulent conveyance. Moreover, Swiss courts cannot recognize foreign judgments filed in Switzerland to collect from Swiss annuities. Swiss insurance law also contains "anti-duress" language. Such wording prohibits the forced return of annuity assets to the jurisdiction of the annuity owner (for attachment by the local creditor). A few other countries, such as the Isle of Man, similarly protect annuities.[89]

---

[88] Marco Gantenbein and Mario Malta, Swiss Annuities and Life Insurance: Secure Returns, Asset Protection, and Privacy, Vol. 400, Wiley Finance, 2008, 86-90, Articles 79-81 of the Swiss Insurance Act.

[89] All creditor claims must be brought in the courts of Isle of Man.

4.7   Miscellaneous Exempt Assets in
        Bankruptcy

The federal government excludes certain additional miscellaneous assets from attachment in bankruptcy. As the protections only cover the basics, they are not generally useful to protect wealth. Examples of such exemptions include the following:

- The debtor's interest in a motor vehicle, not exceeding $3,450.[90]

- The debtor's interest in household furnishings, household goods, apparel, appliances, books, animals, crops, or musical instruments, not exceeding $550 per item or $11,525 in the aggregate, to the extent held primarily for the personal, family, or household use of the debtor or a dependent of the debtor.[91]

- The debtor's interest in jewelry, not exceeding $1,450, held primarily by the debtor or a dependent for personal, family, or household use.[92]

- The debtor's interest in any implements, professional books, or tools of the trade, held

---

[90] 11 U.S.C. § 522(d)(2)(2010).
[91] 11 U.S.C. § 522(d)(3) (2010).
[92] 11 U.S.C. § 522(d)(4) (2010).

by the debtor or a dependent, not exceeding $2,175.[93]

- Prescribed health aids for use by the debtor or a dependent.[94]

- Rights to alimony payments.[95]

4.8 Tenancy by the Entirety

Tenancy by the entirety with rights of survivorship ("TBE") is one of three forms of joint property ownership. Available only to married couples, TBE provides legal protections not available to tenants in common or joint tenants (the other two forms of joint ownership).[96] As long as the marital "entireties" of TBE are maintained, each spouse legally owns the entire TBE property.

---

[93] 11 U.S.C. § 522(d)(6) (2010).

[94] 11 U.S.C. § 522(d)(9) (2010).

[95] *Waters v. Lebanese*, 547 So.2d 197 (Fl. 4th DCA 1989), *rev. denied.* 560 So.2d 237 (Fl. 1990).

[96] Tenancy in common is the most common form of shared ownership. The tenancy is formed by two or more people who jointly purchase property. Each owner enjoys a separate fractional (yet undivided) right to possess the entire property. Each fractional interest may be freely sold or given away (during life or via testamentary devise). Co-tenancy interests are unprotected from creditors. Joint tenancy with right of survivorship is similar but much less common because the tenancy is not inadvertent (as the tenants must intentionally title the property "jtwros"). If property is so titled, the interest held by a deceased tenant passes by law to the surviving tenant(s). Although jtwros interests are unprotected from the creditors of each respective debtor/tenant during his or her life, all collection rights end upon the death of the debtor/tenant.

Husband and wife must together agree to transfer TBE property. The interest of only one spouse in TBE property cannot be transferred, given or willed to a third party. Such "undivided" ownership protects the property from creditors of either spouse. Only a joint creditor of both husband and wife may reach TBE property. Upon the death of a spouse, TBE property transfers entirely to the surviving "tenant" (without probate).

TBE status evolved through the English common law to protect a wife's interest in property. TBE created a means of safely transferring wealth to daughters, who (under the common law) could not hold legal title to property. The dowry could neither be (i) sold by the husband (without the consent of his bride) or (ii) attached by creditors of either husband or wife. This remains the case in states which have adopted the TBE common law format. Thus (excluding the IRS or a fraudulent transfer) a creditor of only one spouse cannot reach property held TBE. Chart 4.8 on page 75 illustrates the protective advantage of TBE.

Alaska, Arkansas, Delaware, Florida, Hawaii, Illinois, Indiana, Kentucky, Maryland, Massachusetts, Michigan, Mississippi, Missouri, New Jersey, New York, North Carolina, Oklahoma, Oregon, Pennsylvania, Rhode Island, Tennessee, Vermont, Virginia, Wyoming and Washington D.C. recognize TBE ownership in a variety of common law and statutory forms. The various states differ dramatically regarding both the type of property eligible, the formalities required and the protections attributed to TBE status.

Chart 4.8

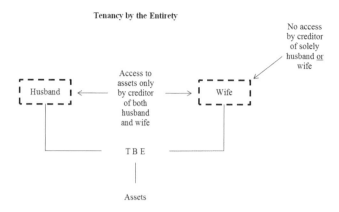

Most states that allow TBE titling limit its use to real estate. Florida, however, allows both personal property and real property to be held TBE. Florida law also presumes that real estate, stock certificates and bank accounts held by a married couple are owned TBE (even if not so titled).[97] A Florida court has also ruled that a presumption of TBE ownership extends to shares of stock held in a jointly titled certificate.[98] Despite any applicable state presumption of TBE ownership, bank accounts, deeds, stock certificates, brokerage statements, and account applications should (if TBE is intended) reflect ownership by husband and wife as "Tenants by the Entirety," or "TBE," to eliminate any doubt.

---

[97] Fl. Stat. § 655.79(1)(2011); Fl. Stat. § 689.115 (2011).

[98] *Cacciatore v. Fisherman's Wharf Realty Ltd. Partnership ex rel. Emalfario Investment Corp.*, 821 So. 2d 1251, 1254 (Fl. 4th DCA 2002).

The legal protections afforded TBE property are not established by simply titling an existing account or piece of real estate "TBE." Unless revised by a particular state law, six "unities" are required to establish TBE status. A summary of the required unities is as follows:

- Unity of possession. Both spouses must hold joint ownership and control.

- Unity of interest. Each spouse must have equal rights and interest in the property or account.

- Unity of time. The title taken to the property by the spouses must be established simultaneously in the same instrument. This requirement is not generally known to the public and can be the "gotcha" in a collection matter. Clients and professionals (such as accountants, financial planners and even attorneys) frequently attempt to protect existing property and accounts titled individually by re-titling the property TBE. This is usually ineffective. New TBE accounts should be funded with cash and securities held in existing individual accounts. Business equity held individually should be redeemed and reissued or replaced with equity in a new successor entity held TBE.

- Unity of title. Both spouses must hold ownership, as reflected in the title to the property (originating from the same instrument).

- <u>Survivorship</u>. The surviving spouse is transferred sole ownership of the property upon the death of a spouse.

- <u>Unity of marriage</u>. The owners must be legally married under the law of the applicable state of residence. Interestingly, accounts held jointly before marriage have been found not to qualify as property held TBE after the wedding. The couple must actually transfer their joint interests to themselves as TBE after the marriage.[99]

The main disadvantage of TBE ownership is joint liability. Both husband and wife are liable for joint obligations arising from, for example, joint ownership of dangerous and/or active assets (such as automobiles, real estate and active businesses). Joint liabilities (in turn) expose other assets held TBE (if not otherwise exempt or sheltered in a protective entity). To avoid joint liability, any dangerous or active assets should be held in an independent entity, such as an LLC or trust. The entity itself may often be held TBE (without exposure to joint liability).

Note that tenancy by the entirety should not be confused with "community property." Community property is an involuntary "joint" ownership status attributed by several states to property owned by one or both spouses. The rules governing community property

---

[99] *In re Caliri*, 347 B.R. 788, 799 (Bankr. M.D. Fl. 2006).

vary from state to state. In a community property state, the debts of either spouse (depending on the state) may be considered owed by both spouses. Although creditors of a single spouse cannot reach TBE property, they may often reach property located in a community property state, without regard to which spouse holds title. In other words, titling property as husband and wife in a community property state generally provides no asset protection benefits.

Arizona, California, Idaho, Louisiana, Nevada, New Mexico, Texas, Washington and Wisconsin are "community property states." Alaska allows spouses to elect either separate property or community property status.[100] All other states are called "separate property" states. Creditors of one spouse in a separate property state have no claim to assets titled in the name of the other spouse. Some states impose exceptions for debt arising from necessary items such as food, but the exceptions are very limited.

The division of marital property in divorce is a related creditor protection issue. Community property is typically split evenly between divorcing spouses. Separate property states tend to treat property acquired during a marriage or intermingled between spouses as "marital property." Marital property is generally split between husband and wife no matter how titled or earned. Prenuptial or postnuptial agreements may, however, be implemented to alter the division of assets. The agreement

---

[100] *See* Ak. Statutes ("AS") 34.77.090(a).

is generally respected by all states, provided that the applicable execution formalities, legal representation and disclosure of assets are properly established. Obviously, prenuptial and postnuptial agreements should be handled by a seasoned attorney familiar with the laws applicable to the couple and their particular assets.

Chapter 5: Fraudulent Transfers

"[Before] judgment (or its equivalent) an unsecured creditor has no rights at law or in equity in the property of his debtor." - *Justice Antonin Scalia (1999)*[101]

It is a common misconception that an individual may legally transfer valuable assets to a friend or relative to avoid attachment by a creditor. Understanding why people seek to avoid collection requires no imagination. Reactionary transfers, however, serve no legal purpose.

Unfortunately, most people consider asset protection only after having become desperate to "hide

---

[101] *Grupo Mexicano de Desarrollo, SA v. Alliance Bond Fund, Inc.* 527, U.S. 308, 330 (1999).

assets" from a creditor. If a debtor could avoid collection by transferring valuable assets when convenient, how could any creditor ever satisfy a judgment? While democratic societies are reluctant to restrict the free transferability of assets, they do allow creditors to recover assets "fraudulently" transferred.

Creditors may reach assets transferred by a debtor to avoid paying a debt. The various fraudulent transfer statutes reflect a clear intent: to invalidate transfers intended to place assets beyond the reach of any existing or reasonably anticipated creditor. The more obvious the abuse associated with a transfer, the more likely the court is to apply the applicable fraudulent transfer law. Even the most established asset protection structures may be undermined if improperly funded. Interestingly, the law[102] typically creates only a remedy to recover assets, not an action against the debtor for money damages.

The "planning" requirement of asset protection originates from the historical rejection of reactionary transfers to thwart legitimate creditors. All U.S. states have adopted legislation allowing a creditor to reach otherwise protected assets. Assets fraudulently transferred may therefore be recovered by means of a suit against the debtor and/or transferee.

The U.S. fraudulent transfer laws do not constrain transfers prior to judgment. Until the creditor wins a

---

[102] *See e.g.,* Ca. Civil Code § 3439.07 "Uniform Fraudulent Transfer Act."

money judgment, the creditor has no legal right to assets of the debtor. The debtor may therefore freely transfer assets before a judgment is entered. However, if a plaintiff succeeds in obtaining a favorable judgment, the new "judgment creditor" can invoke the fraudulent transfer remedy and pursue assets transferred prior to or after the judgment.

Interestingly, although U.S. debtors may freely transfer assets before suffering a judgment (subject to the applicable fraudulent transfer law), several offshore debtor havens limit pre-judgment asset transfers. Several current and former English commonwealth countries allow what is known as a "Mareva" injunction.[103] Pursuant to the injunction, a foreign trustee may not (during litigation), act to impede future creditors' access to trust assets. The trust in question cannot move assets, change jurisdictions or otherwise alter its holdings pending the outcome of litigation.

There is no priority among unsecured creditors to payment from a debtor's assets. Arguably, payment of one unsecured debt before another cannot give rise to a claim of fraudulent transfer. However, paying a home mortgage or a debt to a sibling, before paying an unrelated creditor, may be viewed with judicial scrutiny.

---

[103] *Mareva Compania Naviera SA v. Int'l Bulkcarriers SA* [1975] 2 Lloyd's Rep. 509. A freezing order is a court order preventing a defendant from transferring assets until the outcome of the associated lawsuit is decided.

The determination of fraudulent transfer usually depends on the debtor's intention to avoid a creditor. If the creditor can prove that the debtor transferred title to avoid a debt, the asset may be recovered from the recipient. Creditors unknown to the debtor at the time of the transfer cannot be the subject of intentional avoidance and have no claim to the assets transferred. The earlier the protective transfer is accomplished, the clearer the debtor's intention to plan for unforeseeable claims. Planning remains the key to successful protective transfers. Transfers documented before default or illiquidity and/or made at least partially for business or estate planning reasons are seldom reversed. The key is to plan unforeseen potential creditors out of a remedy.

Let's consider the classic example of the defendant surgeon. The timing of transfers (in relation to medical malpractice) makes clear the intentions of a surgeon. Before surgery, any asset protection is pure planning and therefore outside the realm of intentional fraudulent conveyance. Consider whether a court would find fraudulent intent regarding a protective transfer made immediately after the surgery (based only on an indication of potential malpractice, like excessive bleeding). Intentions become clearer if exposed assets are transferred upon discovery of troubling symptoms. Any protective transfer made after a malpractice claim is obviously intended to avoid the claim.

5.1   History of Fraudulent Transfer Statutes

A review of the historical development of English common law may be helpful in understanding the subtleties of fraudulent transfer law. During the sixteenth century, the Statute of Elizabeth (1571) codified the English common law governing fraudulent transfers. According to the Statute, all conveyances of property made "for any intent or purpose to delay, hinder or defraud creditors... must be deemed and taken to be clearly and utterly void, frustrated and of no effect . . . ."[104] The Statute contained no limitations period within which a creditor must file a fraudulent transfer claim. As a result, creditors were not compelled to start collection proceedings within any fixed period after the transfer.

Early fraudulent transfer cases required proof that the debtor intended to evade the creditor. Establishing a defendant's state of mind can, however, be quite difficult. The courts developed certain objective standards suggesting malicious intent. In *Twyne's Case*, heard by the English Star Chamber in 1601,[105] the court allowed the use of "marks of fraud" to evidence fraudulent intent. These "marks of fraud" included the debtor's receipt of inadequate consideration (for the assets transferred), concealment of assets and transfers resulting in the debtor's insolvency.[106]

---

[104] Statute of Elizabeth, Fraudulent Conveyances Act 1571 (13 Eliz I Cap 5), currently available in UK's Insolvency Act 1986.

[105] *Twyne's Case*, 76 Engl. Rep. 80, 3 Coke 80 (1601).

[106] *Id.*

85

The English colonies (and former colonies) adopted the Statute of Elizabeth (with varying periods of limitation for creditor claims). In the 1980's, several colonies and former colonies such as Nevis, West Indies, enacted short statutes of limitation (barring fraudulent transfer claims not filed within periods as short as one year of the transfer).[107] The offshore trust industry began to flourish around the same period, due in part to such foreign statutes quickly barring fraudulent transfer claims.

Short filing periods are not unique to foreign jurisdictions. For example, Nevada's two year statutory period is the shortest in the U.S.[108] Most states enforce laws similar to the Statute of Elizabeth, but with a 4 to 10 year period of limitations.

Fraudulent transfer remedies were first enacted into statute in the U.S. in 1918 when six states adopted the Uniform Fraudulent Conveyance Act ("UFCA").[109] With a handful of exceptions, the states have adopted the subsequent Uniform Fraudulent Transfers Act ("UFTA"). The two Acts are generally similar. All states except Maryland, New York, Tennessee, Wyoming and the U.S. Virgin Islands have implemented the UFTA. The

---

[107] Nevis International Exempt Trust Ordinance, "Nevis Trust Ordinance" 1994, as amended, § 24(3)(b)(1994-5).

[108] Nev. Rev. Stat. § 166.170.

[109] Alaska, Kentucky, Louisiana, Maryland, South Carolina, Virginia; see Fraudulent Transfer Act Legislative Fact Sheet, The National Conference of Commissions on Uniform State Laws, available at http://www.nccusi.org/LegislativeFactSheet.aspx?; see Uniform Fraudulent Conveyance Act (1918).

determination of which fraudulent transfer law will apply is influenced by the residence of the transferor, transferee and creditor as well as the location of the property.

Under UFTA, a creditor must bring a fraudulent transfer action no later than (i) four years after the transfer was made or (ii) within one year after the transfer was or could reasonably have been discovered (whenever that may be). Compare the UFTA limitations period with Nevada, where the creditor must bring suit no later than (i) two years after transfer or (ii) six months after discovery.

In light of the open period (pending the creditor's discovery of the transfer), debtors should often notify significant creditors of protective transfers, to start the statutory claims period. Protective transfers otherwise remain exposed until the creditor becomes (or should become) aware that assets have been sheltered. Several foreign debtor havens have eliminated the tolling of the limitations period pending discovery of the transfer.

Creditor remedies include (i) injunction (judicial prohibition) against further transfers and (ii) the imposition of a receivership (appointing an outside party to control the assets). Under the Acts, a creditor alleging fraudulent transfer may sue the debtor/transferor and/or the recipient of the property. Both Acts protect creditors whose debts existed (i) before the transfer ("present creditors") and (ii) after the transfer ("future creditors"). However, not all future creditors are protected.

To be considered a protected "future creditor," the liability must have been reasonably "foreseeable"[110] at the time of the fraudulent transfer. In other words, even though the claimant was not legally a creditor when exposed assets were transferred, something had occurred making an anticipated debt likely. A "future creditor" does not exist (i.e., has no claim) unless the debtor can reasonably expect to incur a future claim or judgment to the claimant at the time of conveyance. Therefore, clients or patients are not entitled to pursue protected assets of a service provider if their claim was not reasonably "foreseeable" at the time of the assets were transferred. Planning for unforeseen claims is the basis for asset protection.

In *Leopold v. Tuttle*, the Pennsylvania Supreme Court defined "future creditor" as a reasonably foreseeable creditor.[111] If a foreseeable creditor (at the time of the asset transfer) later wins a judgment, the creditor has a legal claim to recover the asset previously transferred.[112] The future creditor (who, only after the asset transfer, wins a judgment) is therefore entitled to set aside the

---

[110] *Leopold v. Tuttle*, 549 A.2d 151 154 (Pa. Super. Ct. 1988).

[111] *Id. See also Stauffer* 341 A.2d 236, 245 (1976). The Pennsylvania Supreme Court defined "future creditor" as "one with a legal claim against a person at the time that person makes a conveyance even one that has not yet been reduced to judgment or even filed, is a future creditor who is entitled to set aside the conveyance if he can show it was made with actual intent to hinder, delay or defraud present or future creditors." *Stauffer v. Stauffer*, 341 A.2d 236, 245 (1976).

[112] *Stauffer v. Stauffer*, 341 A.2d 236, 245 (1976).

conveyance if he can prove the debtor's intent to hinder, delay or defraud the future creditor.

In the case of *Stauffer v. Stauffer*, Mr. Stauffer transferred to his wife property owned jointly by the Stauffers, for the consideration of $1. Mr. Stauffer did so after admitting to his wife and brother-in-law that he was having an extramarital affair with Mrs. Stauffer's sister (his brother-in-law's wife). To protect the family home from any lawsuit arising from the affair (later initiated by his brother-in-law), Mr. Stauffer fraudulently conveyed his interest in the home to Mrs. Stauffer. The Supreme Court of Pennsylvania found the transfer to be based on Mr. Stauffer's intention to avoid a foreseeable future creditor and therefore a fraudulent conveyance.[113]

To establish protected "future creditor" status, the creditor must be at least identifiable at the time of transfer. If the creditor was not foreseeable, neither Act applies. Consider the Florida case of *Hurlburt v. Shackleton*.[114] Dr. Shackleton, a Florida physician, transferred assets, titled in his name alone, to himself and his wife, TBE.[115] Dr. Shackleton retitled the assets to eliminate exposure to future malpractice claims, in light of rising malpractice insurance costs. Subsequent to the transfers, Dr. Shackleton was found liable for malpractice damages. When the patient attempted to collect the assets previously transferred, the trial court ruled that the patient was a "possible" (but not "probable") creditor. The trial court

---

[113] *Stauffer v. Stauffer*, 351 A.2d 236, 245 (Pa. 1976).
[114] *Hurlburt v. Shackleton*, 560 So. 2d 1276 (Fl. 1st DCA 1990).
[115] *Id.* at 123-125.

concluded that the patient/judgment holder was not entitled to relief under the Florida Fraudulent Transfer Act. The appellate court made clear that "where the creditor is not in existence at the time of the conveyance, there must be evidence establishing actual fraudulent intent by the one who seeks to have the transaction set aside."[116] The ruling may be interpreted as requiring more than a creditor's status as a patient (or client), to be considered a reasonably expected future creditor. A creditor not identifiable at the time of the transfer is not a protected "future creditor."

5.2   Constructive Fraudulent Intent

Once a collection suit has been timely filed, the creditor may first attempt to prove fraudulent intent "constructively." If a creditor proves constructive fraudulent intent (based on objective evidence), the creditor is not required to show bad intentions. A present or future creditor may prove constructive fraudulent intent by showing that the debtor did not receive (i) "reasonably equivalent value in exchange for the transfer, "[117] and (ii) either

(A)   the debtor was engaged (or about to engage) in a business or transaction for which the debtor's remaining assets were unreasonably small; or

---

[116] *Id.* (citing *Eurovest LTD v. Segall*, 528 So. 2d 482, 483-84 (Fl. 3d DCA 1988)).

[117] Fl. Stat. § 726.101 (2011) "Uniform Fraudulent Transfer Act."

(B)   the debtor intended to incur, or believed (or should have believed) that he would incur, debts beyond his ability to pay.[118]

In other words, creditors (whether existing or only foreseeable at the time of the transfer) may invalidate a transfer by proving that the debtor (i) made the transfer without receiving assets of similar value; and (ii) either transferred an inordinate amount of assets to a business or became unable to pay his debts.[119] Note that (under UFTA) a present creditor (whose claim existed before the transfer) must only prove that the debtor (i) transferred assets without receiving reasonable value and (ii) was or became insolvent at the time of the transfer. The present creditor (as opposed to a foreseeable future creditor) is not required to show that the debtor could not pay his debts, but only that the debtor's debts exceeded his assets.

The first hurdle to prove constructive fraudulent transfer is to show that the debtor received less than the value given up. Gifts obviously fail to establish the receipt of equivalent value. At first blush, the transfer of exposed assets to a protective entity, such as an LLC, in exchange for equity in the entity, arguably constitutes receipt of equal value. Several courts have, however, ruled that the receipt of equity in a protective entity (funded with transferred assets) may not constitute reasonably equivalent value. This is because courts tend to value the debtor's assets from the creditor's perspective. Because

---

[118] *Id.*

[119] Fl. Stat. § 726.101 (2011) "Uniform Fraudulent Transfer Act."

the protected asset received (i.e., equity in the protective entity) is not reachable by creditors, equity received is generally not counted as value for assets transferred.[120] In the determination of solvency (step number two), all debtor liabilities are included but exempt assets are ignored. Transfers for equity in a protected entity may therefore create insolvency and result in a constructive fraudulent transfer.

Interestingly, even if the debtor harbored no intent to avoid a debt, a creditor may invalidate a transfer by proving constructive fraudulent intent. On the other hand, if the debtor either (i) received adequate consideration or (ii) (even if consideration was inadequate) did not overcapitalize a business and continued to pay his debts (and remained solvent), constructive fraudulent intent cannot be proven. In such cases, even a present creditor must prove that the debtor intentionally made the transfer to avoid payment. Therefore, a common asset protection strategy is to remain solvent and liquid. Another strategy is to utilize protective foreign trust law which excludes the remedy of constructive fraudulent transfer.

5.3   Badges of Fraud

If constructive fraudulent transfer is not available, the creditor must prove that the debtor actually intended to

---

[120] *See e.g.* John E. Sullivan, *Future Creditors and Fraudulent Transfers: When a Claimant Doesn't Have a claim, When a Transfer Isn't a Transfer, When Fraud Doesn't Stay Fraudulent, and Other Important Limits to Fraudulent Transfer Law for the Asset Protection Planner*, 22 Del. J. Corp. L. 955 (1997).

evade the creditor. Due to the difficulty of proving intent, UFTA, UFCA and the Statute of Elizabeth look back to the medieval "badges of fraud" for indication of intent. The badges are circumstances the court may consider as indications of intent. No single badge is necessarily given more weight than another. The judge or jury may freely consider the various factors in determining the intent of the debtor. UFTA contains the following non-exclusive list of "badges":

- the transfer was to an "insider," e.g., a relative or close acquaintance of an individual debtor, a director, officer, or controlling shareholder of a corporate debtor, or an entity under common control with a debtor;

- the debtor retained possession or control of the property transferred after the transfer;

- the transfer was disclosed or concealed (another reason to disclose all planning to significant creditors);

- before the transfer, the debtor had been sued or threatened with suit;

- the transfer included substantially all of the debtor's assets;

- the debtor absconded;

- the debtor removed or concealed assets;

- the value of the consideration received by the debtor was not reasonably equivalent to the value of the asset transferred;

- the debtor was insolvent or became insolvent shortly after the transfer was made;

- the transfer occurred shortly before or shortly after a substantial debt was incurred;

- the debtor transferred essential assets of a business to a lienor who (in turn) transferred the assets to an insider of the debtor.

Combining asset protection planning with other non-creditor related planning (such as estate planning or business structuring) may also help establish intentions unrelated to debt avoidance. The badges (indicators) of fraud are not available to future creditors in the UFCA or Statute of Elizabeth jurisdictions.

5.4   Fraudulent Transfers Not Fraud

None of the States nor the U.S. Bankruptcy Code treats a "fraudulent transfer" as actual fraud on a creditor. "Fraudulent transfer" is a technical term describing a transfer made for the purpose of avoiding a creditor. Fraud is distinct and involves misleading someone to take financial advantage. Fraud may constitute a crime or the basis of a civil action for damages.

An interesting aspect of fraudulent transfer law is the general absence of repercussions to the transferor. The "worst case scenario" of a civil fraudulent transfer (outside bankruptcy or a government claim) is that the asset is made available to the creditor. In other words, if an event of liability has occurred, there is typically no legal detriment to causing a fraudulent transfer (or converting an exposed asset to a protected asset). Apart from limited sanctions imposed by a few states and potential liability for costs and attorney fees incurred by the creditor, a fraudulent transfer allows only for the recovery of the asset transferred. Aside from California imposing civil and criminal penalties for certain transfers out of state, and Arizona making fraudulent conveyance a criminal misdemeanor or felony (depending on how the law is interpreted), there is often no significant "downside" to effecting the transfer.[121] In light of the litigation costs to recover assets transferred away from a creditor, assets will often not be pursued. Whether the transfer is the right thing to do is another question.

5.5   Government Claims

Obligations owed to the Federal government are subject to onerous fraudulent transfer rules.[122] Fraudulent transfers away from the U.S. government may be established through diminished evidentiary standards, and, in certain cases, constitute a criminal act. The government has broad powers to reverse and punish the avoidance of

---

[121] Ca. Penal Code § 154; Ar. Rev. Stat. Ann. §§ 44-1211; 44-1217; 13-2205(B).

[122] *See* 28 U.S.C. § 3301 *et. seq.* (2009).

its claims. For example, the U.S. government may void transfers made without receiving reasonably equivalent value or intended to hinder, delay or defraud the government. The six year statute of limitations affords the Federal government ample time to attack a transfer as fraudulent.[123] Fraudulent transfers away from governmental entities (empowered with special statutory collection rights and endless taxpayer financing) should be avoided. Examples of statutes which empower the U.S. government and the states to collect debts are as follows:

- <u>Acts to Evade or Defeat Collection</u>: It is a felony to willfully attempt in any manner to evade or defeat the collection of a Federal tax. The transferor may face fines of not more than $100,000 (for individuals) and $500,000 (for corporations) and not more than five years in prison or both, together with the cost of prosecution.[124]

- <u>Obstruction or Impeding</u>: It is a felony to obstruct or impede the due administration of the Federal Internal Revenue Code including impeding the collection of tax owed.[125]

- <u>Omnibus Crime Control Act</u>: It is a crime to conceal or otherwise hinder governmental and

---

[123] Federal Debt Collection Procedures Act, 28 U.S.C. § 3306(b), *see also* 28 U.S.C. § 3201 (2010) "Federal Debt Collection Procedure Act."

[124] IRC §§ 7201 & 7206(4) (2008); 26 U.S.C. §§ 7201, 7206(4).

[125] IRC § 7212 (2008).

quasi-governmental agencies from collection of moneys owed.[126]

- Money Laundering: It is a crime to commit money laundering, which is the concealment of the nature or origin of funds through criminal or fraudulent acts.[127]

- The Bankruptcy Code: Any person who (i) conceals a debtor's assets, (ii) receives the debtors' assets fraudulently, or (iii) transfers or conceals assets on behalf of a corporation, intending to defeat the Bankruptcy Code, may be sentenced to five years in prison.[128]

- Fraud on the United States: This statute makes it a felony to conspire to commit any offense against the United States or to defraud the United States, or any of its agencies. The government must prove (i) an agreement between two people, (ii) a scheme to defraud the U.S., and (iii) an overt act committed in furtherance of the agreement. Convictions have been based on fraudulent transfers including the depletion of corporate assets prior to bankruptcy.[129]

---

[126] Omnibus Crime Control and Safe Streets Act of 1968, Publ. L. 90-351, June 19, 1968, 82 Stat. 197, 42 U.S.C. § 3711.

[127] 18 U.S.C. § 1956.

[128] 18 U.S.C. §§ 152(A)(1),(5),(7) (2009).

[129] 18 U.S.C. § 371; *U.S. v. Switzer*, 252 F. 2d 139 (2nd Cir. 1958).

- California Criminal Statutes: California state criminal laws may apply to acts that hinder the collection of state debts.[130]

5.6   Bankruptcy Code

A general discussion of fraudulent transfers made prior to bankruptcy may be helpful in understanding how to shelter assets (even as part of an attempt to discharge indebtedness). The Federal Bankruptcy Code allows the courts to disregard any transfer made within two years of bankruptcy, if made with the intent to hinder, delay or defraud any present or future creditor. In addition to traditional fraudulent transfer remedies, the 2005 Bankruptcy Act also imposes a broad ten year look back period on transfers made for asset protection purposes.[131] Specifically, the bankruptcy trustee can reverse any transfer to a "self-settled" asset protection trust or "similar device", if made within the ten year period prior to bankruptcy (with the intent to avoid a creditor).[132]   If possible, the debtor should wait beyond the two (or ten) year fraudulent transfer window before filing for a "fresh start."

The bankruptcy trustee may also invalidate any transfer as a "constructive" fraudulent transfer, without having to prove actual intent (similar to the civil court action described in Section 5.3). If the debtor received less than reasonable value for property transferred and was

---

[130] *See e.g.* Ca. Penal Code § 531.

[131] 11 U.S.C. § 522(o).

[132] 11 U.S.C. § 548(e)(1)(C).

(at the time of transfer) (i) insolvent, (ii) overcapitalized a business or transaction, or (iii) intended to incur unaffordable debts, then the trustee may reach the assets transferred without further inquiry. If constructive fraudulent transfer cannot be proven, the bankruptcy court will consider the "badges of fraud" as proof of the debtor's "fraudulent" intent.

5.7 Bankruptcy Cases

Although the number of bankruptcy filings constitutes only a fraction of the suits filed each year, bankruptcy courts hear only collection matters. Consequently, bankruptcy is viewed as a window into how state courts will rule on collection issues. One exposure regarding the development of bankruptcy case law is the tendency of bankruptcy judges to ignore applicable statutory or contractual protections otherwise governing the fraudulent transfer issue. For example, the bankruptcy court has ignored applicable foreign law and applied local law, to eliminate the effectiveness of several offshore trusts.

In 1989, Larry Portnoy established an offshore trust in Jersey (Channel Islands), naming himself as primary beneficiary. Mr. Portnoy transferred his assets to the trust, in light of the impending failure of his business and associated default on guaranteed debt. Mr. Portnoy also deposited his annual salary and transferred his wife's bank account to the trust. The bankruptcy court found the conveyances "fraudulent" and refused to exempt Mr. Portnoy's wages from the bankruptcy estate. The court applied New York law to the offshore trust, to expose trust assets (despite the trust requiring the application of Jersey law).[133]

In another colorful case, Stephen Lawrence, a New York derivatives trader, defaulted on a margin obligation owed to the now defunct brokerage house, Bear Stearns.[134] Lawrence failed to pay Bear Stearns as a result of the 1987 stock market crash. Just prior to an over $20,000,000 arbitration award to Bear Stearns, Mr. Lawrence fraudulently transferred his liquid assets to an asset protection trust in Jersey. Lawrence soon moved the Jersey trust to Mauritius, an island nation in the Indian Ocean, and filed bankruptcy.

Aside from the obvious mistake of failing to do any planning, Mr. Lawrence made two tactical missteps. First, he failed to consider purchasing a home in Florida. The Florida homestead exemption shelters even funds otherwise subject to the Florida Fraudulent Transfer Act. Second, Mr. Lawrence filed for bankruptcy in 1997.

Lawrence (or his attorneys) underestimated the power of the bankruptcy court and was evasive during bankruptcy proceedings. Although bankruptcy is a means of discharging indebtedness, the debtor must "come clean" and disgorge unprotected assets. Bankruptcy courts have broad federal collection powers to apply substance over form. While state courts are generally bound by limited

---

[133] *In re Portnoy*, 201 B.R. 685 (Bankr. S.D. N.Y. 1996).

[134] *In re Lawrence*, 227 B.R. 907 (Bankr. S.D. Fl. 1998), *aff'd* 279 F. 3d 1294 (11th Cir. 2002).

creditor rights, federal bankruptcy courts often successfully ignore state and offshore laws to satisfy creditor claims. The court found Mr. Lawrence dishonest and his inability to turn over trust assets self induced. The court denied discharge of Mr. Lawrence's debts, based on his intent to avoid the Bear Stearns' obligation.

Mr. Lawrence refused to comply with the court order to turn over trust assets. The court actually sent Mr. Lawrence to jail pending payment of the debt. The court incarcerated Mr. Lawrence for contempt for refusing to "repatriate" assets protected offshore. In 2006, after Mr. Lawrence had spent more than six years in prison, he was released, based on the federal court's determination that imprisonment would not coerce the return of trust assets.

We learn from *Lawrence* that planning for a rainy day (in Lawrence's case, Black Monday, 1987) avoids the fraudulent transfer issue. Without a fraudulent transfer, courts are reluctant to ignore domestic and foreign asset protection planning. In fact, successful breach of an asset protection plan almost always involves some permutation of fraudulent transfer.

Chapter 6: Choice of Law

"Foreign trusts are often designed to assist the settlor in avoiding being held in contempt of a domestic court while only feigning compliance with the court's orders ... ." –
Judge Charles Wiggins (1999)[135]

The determination of which law governs the rights of a creditor to reach a debtor's assets is primarily based on two factors. First, the state of residence of the defendant determines which assets are statutorily exempt from creditors. Second, the law of the state or nation of

---

[135] *FTC v. Affordable Media, LLC*, 179 F. 3d 1228, 1240 (9th Cir. 1999).

organization generally protects equity and assets in business entities and trusts.

One of the most powerful elements of asset protection planning is the right to choose from the "buffet" of asset protection entities offered by each state and abroad. Although availing oneself of a specific exemption statute (to protect a particular asset) requires residency in the applicable state, formation of an entity is not limited to residents of the organizing state or foreign country. Entities are available to anyone, provided that certain organizational and maintenance requirements are satisfied. For instance, a universal requirement of corporations and LLCs across the globe is that each establish and maintain a "registered agent" in the jurisdiction of organization (to receive legal service). Once the entity is organized in the desired jurisdiction, the residency of the owner or beneficiary should become irrelevant to the protections offered by the entity.

The U.S. Constitution supports the premise that contracting parties may choose the law governing their agreement. The Contracts Clause[136] prohibits states from enacting laws infringing the ability of parties to contract. The general rule is that the choice of law (reflected in entity organizational documents) applies.[137] A notable exception is that the law of the locality of real estate may govern the property.[138] Proper drafting (clearly

---

[136] U.S. Const. art. I, § 10.

[137] Restatement (Second) Conflicts of Law § 187 (1) (2) (1971).

[138] *Id.* at § 187 (3).

establishing the applicable law) should eliminate the choice of law issue (except arising from real estate).

A few creditors have successfully argued to the contrary, leaving the judge to determine which state (or foreign) law governs the collection action. Creditor arguments tend to rely on ambiguity in the Contracts Clause, the "choice of law" rules of the state with jurisdiction over the case and public policy, to create what is known as a "conflict of law." Conflict of law principles allow the presiding court to potentially disregard the law chosen by a trust grantor or founder of a business entity. Failure of a trial court to respect the applicable choice of law (contained in organizational documents) is uncommon outside bankruptcy.[139]

An issue relevant to the "choice of law" is the "internal affairs doctrine." Each U.S. state and many offshore jurisdictions offer a variety of trusts and business entities with different organizational requirements. Corporations formed in Florida, for instance, require that the initial board of directors be listed in the Articles of Incorporation. No such requirement is imposed on corporations formed in Delaware or Nevada. Also, some organizational statutes are substantially more protective of shareholders, LLC members, partners and trust beneficiaries than others. Pursuant to the internal affairs doctrine, the laws governing the internal operations and structure of an entity are those of the state of organization.

---

[139] *See* Engel, Barry S., *Asset Protection Planning Guide*, 247-251, (CCH Inc., Chicago, 2nd ed.) (2005).

Allowing courts to randomly apply local law to an entity formed in a different state would create uncertainty. To avoid instability, each jurisdiction typically requires application of the law of the organizing state to "internal affairs" (regarding corporate organizational matters, internal operations and the liability of officers, directors, members and transferees). States adopting the internal affairs doctrine respect the governance laws of the state where the entity in question was organized. Although rulings providing any guidance are sparse, protections likely governed by the internal affairs doctrine include the "corporate veil" (protecting entity owners from business creditors, covered at Section 7.1) and charging order protection (limiting creditors of LLC members and partners to company distributions, covered at Section 7.2).

The various states have adopted varying degrees of the internal affairs doctrine. For example, Delaware does not recognize any exceptions to the internal affairs doctrine. California law, however, includes substantial exceptions.[140] The goal is to utilize the most protective entity available and limit the potential application of unintended law. Amazingly, relatively few business people, investors or even attorneys, ever consider the issue.

---

[140] *Friese v. Superior Ct.,* 36 Cal. Rptr. 3d 558, 565-71 (Cal. App. 4 Dist. 2005). Moreover, the Delaware courts have refused to recognize California's statutory exception to the internal affairs doctrine, Ca. Corp. Code § 25502.5; *see Vantage-Point Venture Partners 1996 v. Examen, Inc.* 871 A. 2d 1108 (Del. Supr. 2005).

A related matter involves the enforcement of judgments among the states. Any individual state court ruling may be enforced throughout the United States, pursuant to the "Full Faith and Credit" clause of the U.S. Constitution. The text of the Full Faith and Credit Clause[141] is as follows:

> Full faith and credit shall be given in each state to the public acts, records, and judicial proceedings of every other state. And the Congress may by general laws prescribe the manner in which such acts, records, and proceedings shall be proved, and the effect thereof.

The Constitution requires all U.S. courts to enforce the judgments of all other states. The Constitution does not, however, mention the "laws" or "statutes" of other states. Courts may, under certain circumstances, apply the law of their home state in determining the validity of out-of-state and foreign creditor protections. A poorly prepared asset protection plan could become subject to the substantive law of a different (creditor friendly) state.

An additional issue raised by the choice of law question is: Which state court will interpret the law? Jurisdiction of the particular court to hear the case may be established in the contract between the parties. Without a contract, the court considers the relationships or contacts of the parties to a particular state. Jurisdiction often falls

---

[141] U.S. Const. art. IV, § 1.

clearly in one state if, for example, all parties, the debt, the entity, etc., are based in that state. If, however, the litigants, contracts, trustees, etc. are based in a variety of states (and the parties have not contractually agreed to a jurisdiction), doubt as to the applicable judicial jurisdiction may result in a "race for judgment."

If a creditor has the opportunity (based on the contacts of the parties) to file suit in a creditor friendly state, the judgment obtained will likely become enforceable in every state. Depending on the facts of the case, a debtor facing collection in a state favoring creditors may become subject to a liberal interpretation of his asset protection plan. This could occur even though the law written into the asset protection plan was established in a different (debtor friendly) state. An adverse interpretation of a particular state's protections may also influence other state courts, even the courts of the state whose debtor friendly laws govern the plan.

In organizing a legal entity, whether a trust or a business, the documents should clearly establish the choice of law applicable to the entity, its owners, managers, beneficiaries and trustees. The jurisdiction of the court to hear any dispute involving the protective aspects of an entity may also be chosen in the trust, LLC operating agreement, partnership agreement, etc. As the law chosen in a governing document is almost always respected, the drafter should implement the most protective law. The documents should, under certain circumstances, also allow for transfer of jurisdiction (and governing law) in the event that a more protective option becomes available.

6.1 Offshore Conflicts of Laws—The Basis for Foreign Planning

6.1.1 Advantages of Foreign Planning

If properly integrated, foreign protections bolster almost any asset protection structure. Although usually more expensive than domestic planning, foreign planning should be considered for several reasons.

First, foreign planning contemplates protecting assets offshore. Assets held in an offshore debtor haven are very difficult to reach. Courts govern only people and property within their respective jurisdictions. A court's "jurisdiction" is defined by the geographical scope of its power, based on the applicable state or federal constitution. A U.S. court cannot enforce a U.S. judgment by attaching property held outside the geographical limit of its power. Without jurisdiction, domestic courts cannot reach foreign property or control foreign trustees/managers to satisfy U.S. debts.

Placing assets offshore also tends to discourage creditors from spending the time and money required to win a U.S. judgment (collection of which is contingent on reaching unavailable assets). Foreign trustees and managers ignore U.S. rulings and may, at any time, shift assets to a new jurisdiction. Less than three percent of creditors attempt to satisfy their judgments with offshore assets.[142] Even when foreign assets are pursued, the cases are often settled for a small portion of the judgment.

Conversely, the advantages of offshore planning are weakened by funding a foreign entity with U.S. assets. If assets are held in the U.S., the court may be tempted to ignore the protective foreign law governing the entity/owner. Although the legality of disregarding applicable law is questionable (especially in the absence of a fraudulent transfer) the issue should be considered. For instance, a U.S. asset protection trust (discussed in Chapter 3) may, for domestic assets, be a prudent alternative to a foreign trust because it may create less judicial cynicism.

Forced repatriation of foreign assets coerced through incarceration is very rare outside of bankruptcy or government claims.[143] The risk of incarceration to repatriate foreign assets (to pay a U.S. judgment) should, however, be considered. Note that, even in the event of a repatriation order, Mr. Lawrence and the Andersons (discussed at Section 6.5) were able to retain foreign assets (after enduring judicial incarceration).

Second, debtor haven courts are typically prohibited from respecting U.S. judgments. Debtor friendly states, such as Cook Islands, Luxembourg, and Nevis, do not recognize the enforceability of U.S.

---

[142] Alan Northcott, *Asset Protection for Business Owners and High-Income Earners: How to Protect What You Own from Lawsuits and Creditors* (Atlantic Publishing Groups, Inc., Ocala, Florida), (2009).

[143] *Id.* at 154.

judgments against trusts formed in such countries. Courts in debtor friendly countries must actually ignore judgments obtained in the U.S. Debtor havens require that the underlying lawsuit be again litigated in the governing jurisdiction. To collect assets in a debtor friendly country, the U.S. creditor must again prove the case for damages in the foreign court. Only then may such U.S. creditor record a "local" judgment to attach exposed assets in the offshore jurisdiction. The odds of a successful suit offshore are extremely low, considering the failure of the government funded FTC (in *Anderson*, p. 135), Bear Stearns (in *Lawrence*, p. 43) and a large group of condo owners (in *South Orange*, p. 133) to collect in Mauritius and the Cook Islands.

Contrast the larger and older western countries which have signed treaties with the United States, permitting the mutual filing and enforcement of judgments. Judgment treaties allow collection of judgments obtained in one member country in all other member countries. Treaties provide for judgment reciprocity similar to that between each of the fifty United States under the Full Faith and Credit Clause of the U.S. Constitution. For example, Canada and England have enacted legislation allowing the "domestication" of U.S. judgments. Once domesticated, any U.S. federal or state judgment becomes enforceable in Canada and England (at marginal cost).

The absence of a judgment treaty with the foreign jurisdiction could potentially create one weakness. Unlike the constitutional obligation between states to respect the judgments of all states, state courts may consider the absence of a treaty obligation an invitation to disregard foreign law. For example, in the case of *Hilton v. Guyot*, the Supreme Court of the United States refused to enforce a judgment by a French court based on the fact that France once refused to enforce U.S. judgments.[144] Whether the absence of a mutual enforcement treaty creates a practical disadvantage is, however, speculative.

Note that the doctrine of comity is also respected by the larger western countries. Comity is the idea that other legal systems are presumed to make fair and accurate legal determinations. Comity leads to the enforcement of foreign judgments (even in the absence of a treaty). Jurisdictions which grant comity to foreign judgments should be avoided for foreign trusts, corporations and LLCs. The United States and Britain are among the countries which recognize the doctrine of comity.

In addition to U.S. judgments, document disclosure orders, subpoenas for evidence, etc., often cannot be enforced in debtor havens. Necessary witnesses, trustees, managers or other parties cannot be forced to attend depositions or trials or to produce documentation. As a result, favorable offshore law may be utilized to establish friendly (uncooperative) management by a foreign entity or individual. Moreover, foreign financial institutions (along with the trustee or manager) will ignore any U.S. judgment, pursuant to the terms of the governing document.

---

[144] *Hilton v. Guyot*, 159 U.S. 113 (1895).

In contrast, U.S. financial institutions obey domestic judgments without question. A U.S. court ruling to seize domestic assets will always be respected by the domestic bank or brokerage house holding the funds (regardless of whether the account is owned by a protective foreign entity). Even if the order violates the terms of the applicable trust or operating agreement, the assets will be released.

The third advantage of foreign planning is that the collection law of debtor haven countries inhibits creditor success. If a U.S. creditor manages to file suit, win a trial and establish a judgment in a foreign country, offshore collection proceedings may be initiated. Foreign trusts, limited partnerships and LLCs typically benefit from protections which emulate the strongest protections available in the U.S. Laws common to debtor friendly countries may employ bond requirements (for bringing a collection claim), heightened burdens of proof, the clearest LLC charging order protection, language saddling the creditor with the debtor's litigation costs (if the collection suit is unsuccessful) and shortened limitations periods to initiate collection or to file a fraudulent transfer claim. Correspondingly, stringent foreign evidentiary rules and civil procedure also tend to favor the debtor.

Debtor friendly jurisdictions require prompt pursuit of collections claims. Shortened claims periods promote the secret funding of foreign trusts and LLCs, even after an event of liability or suit has been brought in the U.S. Assets will remain under the protection of the foreign state unless the creditor initiates litigation in the foreign jurisdiction before the passage of the limitations period. This places a U.S. creditor at a distinct disadvantage. While the U.S. litigation wears on, the period of limitations (to file suit abroad) is closing (usually without any warning to the creditor). The window of opportunity to file suit abroad closes within a short time of discovering the defendant's liability or fraudulent transfer.

Unlike U.S. statutes of limitation to recover assets fraudulently transferred, foreign limitation periods are not suspended until the creditor has knowledge of the transfer. The Nevis Trust statute, for instance, limits the period for fraudulent transfer claims against trusts to the earlier of (i) two years after accrual of (a basis for) the legal claim or (ii) one year after the protective transfer.[145] The likelihood of the creditor quickly identifying valuable assets moved offshore during the initial phases of U.S. litigation is remote.

As noted, several debtor havens also require that the plaintiff challenging a protective transfer prove his case "beyond a reasonable doubt." This burden of proving a debtor's intent to avoid the creditor is substantially greater than the American "more likely than not" standard.

There are several additional practical reasons to implement foreign protections. For example, the popular debtor friendly nations derive significant revenue from trust, LLC and international business company filings. As

---

[145] Nevis International Exempt Trust Ordinance, 1994, as amended, § 44(2).

a result, offshore courts have historically favored debtors, to avoid legal precedent leading to loss of government revenue.[146]

Financial and psychological advantages are also inherent in offshore planning. Foreign LLCs and trusts create a psychological obstacle to collection. Plaintiff attorneys practicing in personal injury, collections, or similar areas are always encouraged by the availability of immediately liquid and unprotected assets. Without the prospect of "low hanging fruit" (such as liability insurance or unprotected cash), collection will require substantial time and effort.

An exotic entity will discourage (and often completely frustrate) a trial or collection attorney pressured to find payment in as little time as possible. The smaller the potential recovery, the less time and resources the plaintiff's lawyer can gainfully devote to attempting to earn his percentage of the judgment. Small judgments involving assets held in a protective entity (especially a foreign entity) are often abandoned before the attorney would even consider researching the strength of the applicable protections.

Foreign collection actions are astronomically expensive. Pursuing the assets of a foreign entity requires tax, trust and international law experts. The collection action requires an exhaustive analysis of the jurisdictional

---

[146] *In re Brown*, 1996 WL 33657614 (Bankr. D. AK. 1996) (amended memorandum decision).

and choice of law issues. A foreign attorney licensed in the offshore haven must be retained for any litigation and to assess any foreign structure. Also, several offshore jurisdictions require the party losing the litigation to pay all legal fees and other expenses of the winner.[147]

Diversity in foreign planning is particularly effective because the research, legal, filing and expert fees increase exponentially with the use of multiple jurisdictions. Such costs may not be easily quantifiable. The unknown is a very powerful psychological deterrent. The practical obstacles associated with reaching assets offshore may (by themselves) justify establishing foreign trusts, LLCs and partnerships funded abroad.

6.1.2 Specific Offshore Trust Advantages

Several offshore debtor havens enacted trust legislation in the 1980s allowing the settlor to act as a protected trust beneficiary.[148] As a result, offshore spendthrift trusts are often funded for the benefit of the individual founder of the trust. Such trusts are known as "self-settled" asset protection trusts. Foreign asset protection trusts offer particular asset protection benefits and eliminate the anti-American obstacles associated with banking and investing abroad. Although not advisable, the settlor may also act as trustee, with control over trust

---

[147] Nevis International Exempt Trust Ordinance § 31 (1994, as amended); Cook Islands International Trust Act (1984).

[148] Gideon Rothschild, Daniel Rubin, *Has Offshore Trust Litigation Spoiled the Fun? Recent Decisions Regarding Offshore Trusts*, available at http://mosessinger.com/articles/files/offshoretrust.htm.

assets (not allowed with domestic asset protection trusts, discussed at Section 3.2).

Several jurisdictions have tailored their trust statutes to establish burdensome creditor obstacles while providing flexibility to the settlor. Such statutes typically exclude all other trust law from application to any trust established in the haven. Such provisions inhibit U.S. or other foreign courts from attempting to apply their creditor friendly law.

Trust statutes in Nevis and the Cook Islands inhibit creditor claims by increasing the cost of filing suit.[149] Both countries prohibit contingency legal fee arrangements (where legal fees become due only upon collection). Prohibiting contingency fees forces the claimant to pay a retainer and hourly legal billing. Also, the claimant must post an expensive bond in Nevis to file suit. The bond insures that the plaintiff will honor its obligation to pay the legal fees of the debtor, if the claimant fails to collect.

It may also be difficult to prove that a debtor made a fraudulent transfer to an offshore trust. In the U.S., a fraudulent transfer may be proven by "a preponderance of evidence" that a fraudulent transfer occurred. In other words, if the claimant can prove that it is "more likely than not" that assets were fraudulently transferred, the assets may be attached. Several debtor havens (including Nevis

---

[149] Nevis International Exempt Trust Ordinance § 31 (1994, as amended); Cook Islands International Trust Act (1984).

and Cook Islands) have raised the evidence bar by requiring proof of fraudulent transfer "beyond a reasonable doubt."

The Nevis and the Cook Islands trust legislation essentially eliminates fraudulent transfer claims regarding trust assets contributed by a solvent grantor. If the grantor was solvent after funding a trust in either jurisdiction, the grantor is considered to lack the intent to avoid the creditor. Creditors of a solvent grantor cannot therefore invoke the fraudulent transfer remedy to reach trust assets.[150] Moreover, even if the debtor is proven insolvent after transfer, the creditor must still prove that the debtor transferred assets to the trust with the intention of avoiding the creditor.

The Belize Trusts Act contains no remedy for fraudulent transfers. Belize law eliminates any creditor right (for any period) to recover assets transferred to a Belize trust (even if transferred to avoid a creditor).[151]

In the case of *Riechers v. Riechers*, a New York lower court respected the choice of law provision in a Cook Islands self-settled trust, established by a urologist.[152] The court did, however, claim jurisdiction over Dr. Riechers (personally) in the divorce proceeding and considered trust assets in its division of marital property. Although Mrs. Riechers may access the doctor's

---

[150] Nevis Intl. Exempt Trust Ordinance § 24 (1994, as amended).

[151] Belize Trusts Act, Chp. 202 §1 (7) (2000, as amended).

[152] *Reichers v. Riechers*, 178 Misc. 2d 170, 679 N.Y.S. 2d 233 (1998).

exposed U.S. holdings, trust assets will likely remain protected.

Many foreign (and some domestic) jurisdictions allow for a "trust protector" to be named in the trust. The trust protector is someone appointed in addition to the trustee, to oversee trust operations. A protector may be named to approve distributions and monitor trust accounting and trustee activities. The protector serves as a gatekeeper with the power to remove an unprofessional or overpriced trustee or veto proposed investments and distributions.

A trust protector may be beneficial to U.S. settlors unfamiliar with a foreign trust jurisdiction or the foreign trustee. As an alternative to a U.S. settlor appointing himself as trustee (in control of trust distributions), the settlor may serve as protector of a foreign asset protection trust. As trustee, a settlor exposes trust assets to a collection claim based on the settlor's ability to reach trust assets. As protector, the settlor does not technically control the trust but may generally veto any major action of (or remove) the trustee.

Some of the principal foreign trust benefits offered by several favorable jurisdictions are described in Chart 6.1.2. As you review the chart, note that, unlike domestic asset protection trusts, the foreign jurisdictions do not exclude trust protection from certain creditors (involving, for example, tort claims, familial support and alimony).

Chart 6.1.2

Selected Offshore Asset Protection Trusts
Statutory Characteristics

country	foreign judgments not recognized	settlor may retain some control	statute of limitations to reach trust assets through fraudulent transfer	proof beyond reasonable doubt required to establish fraudulent intent	creditor bears burden of proving fraudulent intent	bond required to litigate	trust remains valid in spite of fraudulent transfer	presumption against fraudulent intent if grantor solvent following funding	binding choice of law
Antigua/Barbuda	✓	✓	✓	✓	✓	✓	✓		✓
Bahamas	✓	✓	✓		✓		✓		✓
Belize	✓	✓	N/A	N/A	N/A		N/A	N/A	✓
Cook Islands	✓	✓	✓	✓	✓		✓	✓	✓
Labuan	✓	✓	✓	✓	✓		✓	✓	✓
Mauritius	✓		✓		✓				✓
Nevis	✓	✓	✓	✓	✓	✓	✓	✓	✓
Saint Vincent & the Grenadines	✓	✓	✓	✓	✓		✓	✓	
Seychelles			✓	✓	✓				✓

The use of offshore entities is (at best) tax neutral. Although foreign protections may be combined with income and estate tax planning, implementing offshore protections does not create any tax planning opportunities. It should also be kept in mind that the U.S. tax compliance and reporting rules regarding foreign trusts, corporations and LLCs are generally more involved and burdensome than the analogous laws governing domestic entities. Foreign structuring should not be attempted "online" or by sending a check to a promoter. Self-help in the foreign arena can compromise protections and have dreadful tax implications.

6.2   Extraordinary Creditor Remedies

There are two types of extraordinary remedies available to creditors attempting to collect assets held by a foreign entity and/or located abroad. Despite the barriers to offshore collection, if the debt is large enough, the creditor sufficiently funded and the protected assets substantial, the creditor may move to (i) "set aside" the foreign trust or corporate entity sheltering U.S. assets and/or (ii) have an order issued to repatriate foreign assets.

The legal action to expose assets in a protective entity (to creditors of the owner) is known as "reverse veil piercing." The name comes from the traditional business creditor remedy of "piercing the corporate veil," i.e., breaking through the entity to the "outside" assets of the owner. Traditional "veil piercing" from inside a business entity, to reach the personal assets of the business owner is reversed when a personal creditor of the owner seeks assets in the owner's LLC, partnership or trust.

Creditors have successfully set aside a protective foreign entity (to reach U.S. assets held by the entity) based on circumstances including: (i) the settlor's retention of absolute control over assets in the entity, (ii) the lack of legal formality associated with entity operations, (iii) the absence of any business purpose of the entity, and (iv) the use of entity funds to pay personal expenses. The legal theories for "reverse veil piercing" (where an entity is liable for the owner's personal debts) include "constructive trust" or "resulting trust." In such cases, the creditor argues that the protective entity is a sham which should be deemed to hold assets for the debtor, making them available to the creditor.

A similar legal strategy for reverse veil piercing is the "alter ego" theory, whereby a protective entity is disregarded as nothing more than an alter ego of the debtor. Alter ego cases historically involve the failure of business owners to operate for business purposes or respect the formalities of the entity. When the debtor blurs the distinction between the legal entity and him or herself, the argument may be made that the corporation, LLC, trust, etc. is nothing more than the "alter ego" of the grantor/founder. The alter ego should (the argument goes) be disregarded, as failing to protect (i) its owner from liabilities of the entity and (ii) its assets from debts of its owner.

One means of proving that a business entity is the "alter ego" of its owner is to show that the entity was created or funded with no business purpose.[153] A business purpose has been established for the following activities: (i) maintaining assets within the family unit,[154] (ii) controlling distributions, (iii) consolidating investments for economies of scale and cost savings, (iv) simplifying annual giving, (vi) avoiding probate and (vii) properly managing partnership assets.[155]

The absence of substantial case law involving legitimate planning suggests that foreign entities are typically respected in favor of the debtor. Nonetheless, particular care should be taken regarding assets located in the U.S., even if held in an offshore entity. Owners must always respect corporate formalities, keep separate books and maintain absolute segregation of financial activities. Family investment partnerships or LLCs (generally founded by a married couple to hold investment assets) should take particular care to keep meticulously segregated books, limit bank account activity to business matters and strictly comply with the managerial terms of any governing documentation.

In cases involving dubious transfers to a foreign trust or LLC, or relinquishment of control over the entity to avoid collection, the presiding judge will invariably be

---

[153] *In re Turner*, 335 B.R. 140, 147 (Bankr. N.D. Cal. 2005), modified 345 B.R. 674 (Bankr. N.D. Cal. 2006).
[154] *Moore v. C.I.R. T.C. Memo 1991-546, 1991 WL 220426 (U.S. Tax Ct.*, 1991), 62 T.C.M. 1128 (1991).
[155] *Bischoff v. Comm'r.*, 69 T.C. 32, 39-41 (1977).

tempted to invalidate an otherwise protective arrangement. The bankruptcy cases (Section 6.3) describe various circumstances leading to judicial disregard of foreign trusts as the "alter ego" of the grantor.

A domestic creditor may also request the court to order repatriation of foreign assets. If the ruling is ignored, the U.S. judge may issue a contempt order to coerce recovery of offshore assets. The effectiveness of an order requiring the debtor to repatriate assets depends on the physical presence of the debtor and the presiding judge's willingness to actually incarcerate the debtor for failing to disgorge foreign assets.

In light of the potential for contempt, an overview of the applicable law may be helpful. Contempt of court is generally defined as "conduct interfering with the administration of justice and punishable by fine or imprisonment."[156] Contempt of court may be either civil or criminal contempt. Acts of civil contempt include willful failure to obey a court order issued for another party's benefit. Civil contempt may be ordered to physically coerce compliance with the court order. The typical sanctions are fines and/or incarceration until compliance with the order. Conversely, criminal contempt is imposed, not to produce a remedy through coercion, but to punish for defiance of a court's judicial authority.

When compliance is impossible, civil contempt is inappropriate (because compliance may not be coerced).

---

[156] *Black's Law Dictionary* 313 (7th ed. 1999).

The U.S. Supreme Court has clarified that U.S. courts may not impose civil contempt as punishment "no matter how reprehensive the conduct" when coercion is impossible. The U.S. Supreme Court has consistently ruled that "impossibility of performance" is a defense to a civil contempt order.[157] The Florida Supreme Court has also confirmed that, because "... incarceration is utilized solely to obtain compliance, it must be used only when the contemnor has the ability to comply."[158]

The *Lawrence* and *Anderson* cases, however, suggest that the impossibility defense will be rejected where impossibility is reactionary and self-serving. If a debtor with control over trust assets self-imposes restrictions on his ability to reach trust assets (to avoid a creditor), the court may jail the debtor (to coerce recovery of trust assets). In *Anderson*, where the FTC attempted to recover funds obtained through a fraudulent telemarketing scheme (discussed in Section 6.5), the court jailed the debtors for six months, rejecting "self-induced impossibility" as a defense to civil contempt.[159] The *Lawrence* court also rejected the defense, despite the Supreme Court precedent to the contrary.[160]

The *Lawrence* case led to a few similar rulings such as *SEC v. Bilzerian*. In *Bilzerian*, a brazenly offensive debtor transferred assets to a Cook Islands Trust after being found liable for $62,000,000 in securities fraud

---

[157] *See e.g. U.S. v. Rylander*, 460 U.S. 752, 758(1983).

[158] *Bowen v. Bowen*, 471 So. 2d 1274, 1277 (Fl. 1985).

[159] *In re Lawrence* 227 B.R. 907, 916 (Bankr. S.D. Fl. 1998).

[160] *Id.*

and failing to provide an accounting of his assets. Bilzerian was incarcerated for several months, pending his release of personal financial and trust information. He was denied the right to challenge a contempt order, even though he could not arguably reach trust assets.[161]

Other contempt cases include *BankFirst v. Legendre*[162] (where a few days of incarceration induced the debtor to cooperate and surrender assets to the bankruptcy trustee); *Eulich v. US*[163] (where a debtor was found in civil contempt for failure to disclose Bahamian trust documents to the IRS and fined $5,000 per day, increased to $10,000 per day after 30 days of non-compliance, with additional fines and incarceration proposed after 45 days; and *SEC v. Solow*[164] (where a federal court incarcerated the debtor for failing to disgorge $3,424,788 from a Cook Islands trust, allegedly obtained as part of a fraudulent trading scheme).

The decisions in the *Lawrence* and subsequent cases arguably invalidate reactionary, self-imposed impossibility as a defense to civil contempt. These cases support the idea that, the greater the degree of control retained by the grantor of a foreign trust, the more tempted the court will be to compel distributions to the creditor. The prudent approach is to establish protective trusts with little or no grantor control over trust distributions.

---

[161] *SEC v. Bilzerian*, 131 F. Supp. 2d 10 (U.S. D.C. 2001).
[162] *BankFirst v. Legendre*, Case No. 5DO2-300 (Florida App. 2002).
[163] *Eulich v. U.S.*, 104 AFTR 2d 6332 (N.D. Tex. 2004).
[164] *SEC v. Solow*, 682 F. Supp. 2d 1312 (S.D. Fl. 2010).

Despite the risk of incarceration in cases of fraudulent transfer and ill-gotten gains, the eventual release of Michael and Denyse Anderson and Mr. Lawrence suggests that (i) incarceration (although potentially substantial) may be of limited duration and (ii) trust assets abroad will likely remain secure. Also, the narrow line of cases involving incarceration of a debtor for contempt suggests that only (i) bankruptcy and (ii) government supported claims are likely to result in the debtor facing jail time (to coerce payment of a civil judgment).

6.3   Public Policy as a Creditor Remedy in Bankruptcy

As discussed in Chapter 4, state residency governs the availability of creditor exemptions protecting particular assets (such as annuities and life insurance). The only requirement for formation of protective foreign trusts and LLCs, on the other hand, is proper documentation. A few creditors have avoided the application of protective offshore law, based on a series of bankruptcy cases replacing foreign protections with the law of the debtor's U.S. domicile. Such cases rely on "public policy" and add instability to the already unpredictable body of law dealing with conflicts of law.

A U.S. court, presented with a malicious or negligent trust beneficiary, is faced with a quandary. Should the court (i) respect the clearly applicable law governing a trust or LLC (rendering the creditor's judgment worthless) or (ii) fabricate a creditor remedy (to give credence to a state judgment or fund a bankruptcy estate)?

Several bankruptcy judges have answered the question by ignoring the terms of the foreign trust and relying on "public policy" to apply the trust law of the debtor's U.S. residence. Emboldened by the supremacy of federal bankruptcy law (over state law), a few judges have ignored protective foreign trusts by applying the law of the debtor's residence. If the debtor's domicile does not recognize domestic asset protection trusts (i.e., trusts protective of a settlor/beneficiary), the application of such state law to a foreign trust will expose trust assets benefitting the settlor. The settlor of any self-settled trust should carefully consider the risks of bankruptcy. The issue of residency (regarding the choice of law) has become quite significant in the foreign trust arena.

The U.S. bankruptcy court has converted what is generally viewed as a straightforward determination of applicable law (based on the terms of the trust) into a results oriented "public policy" manipulation. The creditor argues that the trust should be ignored, thereby requiring the applicable trust law to be that of the debtor's U.S. residence. If the facts of the case are sufficiently egregious, the bankruptcy court tends to apply local law, to allow attachment of trust assets. Insolvency (exposing the debtor to bankruptcy) has therefore become a very risky proposition regarding foreign trust assets.

Foreign trust law has been ignored for such reasons as the grantor's personal use of the trust as an "alter ego," rather than as a distinct legal entity.[165]   The alter ego theory has historically been implemented by business creditors to breach the "veil" protecting shareholders from business liabilities (due to a failure to maintain corporate formalities). The bankruptcy court has transformed the claim into a means of disregarding foreign trusts. When the grantor (as opposed to an unrelated trustee) exercises complete control over a foreign trust (even if in compliance with the applicable foreign trust law), the "look and feel" of the trust arrangement may be lost. According to the bankruptcy court, when the grantor may simply pull money from the trust, the existence of a distinct trust entity becomes vague and unsupportable. If the settlor/beneficiary can freely treat the trust as a personal bank account, without trustee supervision or accounting, the court may ignore trust protections. Local trust assets may then be attached by creditors of the grantor and repatriation orders enforced through imprisonment for civil contempt.

The absence of an unrelated trustee may invite a bankruptcy court to employ a "substance over form" argument to apply local law and eliminate offshore protections. Self-settled trusts benefitting a grantor who appoints himself as trustee may not therefore be relied on in bankruptcy. A potential alternative is the appointment of the settlor as trust protector, with limited authority to replace an unrelated trustee.

---

[165] *In re Brown* (*Higashi v. Brown*), 1996 WL 33657614 (Bankr. D. AK.) (amended memo decision).

In the 1996 case of *In re Brown*, the bankruptcy court ruled that assets held in a Belize trust were subject to creditor claims because the trust was a mere "alter ego" of the debtors.[166] The debtors had transferred their assets to a Belize trust long before a later tort claim but retained substantial control of trust assets (which remained in the U.S.). The court expressed concern that "fundamental policies" of Alaskan and American law would not be served by applying the law of the trust's origin. The court ruled that the trust should be ignored because the debtors enjoyed sole control over trust assets. The court disregarded the trust as a "sham" and found the law of the Alaska litigation forum controlling (invalidating the Belize trust law protections).[167]

The bankruptcy court seems particularly interested in allowing creditor claims against foreign trusts funded as part of an abusive or deceptive scheme. Bankruptcy rulings to attach foreign trust assets typically involve fraudulent transfers or an otherwise deceptive debtor. Bankruptcy courts have also declared trust assets fair game when found after the debtor failed to disclose their existence.

As noted on p. 99, in the 1996 case of *In re Portnoy*,[168] Larry Portnoy funded a Jersey (Channel Islands) trust just before the imminent default on corporate debt he personally guaranteed. He then filed bankruptcy

---

[166] *In re Brown* (*Higashi v. Brown*), 1996 WL 33657614 (Bankr. D. Ak.).

[167] *Id.*

[168] *In re Portnoy* 201 B.R. 685 (Bankr. S.D. N.Y. 1996).

to discharge the guarantees. Mr. Portnoy failed to disclose the foreign asset protection trust or his salary to the court. The creditor argued that Mr. Portnoy's trust should be disregarded as his "alter ego" because of his concealment and control over trust assets. Mr. Portnoy claimed that trust assets could not be reached under the law of Jersey and that all of his debts, including the guarantee, should be discharged. The court found that Mr. Portnoy had lied in claiming himself financially ruined by cancer treatments. The court applied rough justice to expose all trust assets to Mr. Portnoy's creditors. The court did so by ruling that the law of New York (Mr. Portnoy's residence) governed the trust. The court concluded that:

> The trust, the beneficiaries, and the ramifications of Portnoy's assets being transferred into trust have their most significant impact in the United States. In addition, I believe that application of Jersey's substantive law would offend strong New York and federal bankruptcy policies if it were applied.[169]

The bankruptcy court also hinted that Mr. Portnoy engaged in a fraudulent conveyance to the offshore trust. There was, however, no apparent legal basis to disregard the Jersey law written into the trust (apart from generally offending New York law and bankruptcy principles). A potentially more effective bankruptcy strategy would have been to disclose all trust holdings, leaving some assets

---

[169] *Id.*

131

outside the trust, as the so-called "sacrificial lamb," to claim a "fresh start."

In the 1998 case, *In re Brooks*, the bankruptcy court ruled on whether to apply local Connecticut law or the trust law of Bermuda and Jersey.[170]   In 1990, Mr. Brooks transferred his stock certificates (via his wife) to an offshore "self-settled" trust organized in the Isle of Jersey (purportedly for estate planning purposes). One year later, Mr. Brooks was forced into bankruptcy. The creditor argued that trust assets were available to creditors because the trusts were "self-settled and invalid as a matter of law." The debtor claimed that the trusts were "not property of the estate because they are enforceable spendthrift trusts." Ignoring any legal analysis, the court ruled that "on the basis of public policy considerations...the enforceability of the spendthrift provisions of the trusts is determined under Connecticut law."[171]   Connecticut law does not protect self-settled trusts. Thus, the Brooks court included all trust assets in the bankruptcy estate.

A few interesting facts were cited by the court. The primary beneficiary of each trust was the settlor, with the right to receive all income. The court referred to the creation of the trusts as a "scheme."[172]   Also, the trusts were funded in 1990 and an involuntary bankruptcy petition was filed against the debtor the following year.[173] Although not articulated, the court likely considered the

---

[170] *In re Brooks*, 217 B.R. 98 (Bankr. D. Conn. 1998).

[171] *Id.* at 102.

[172] *Id.* at 103.

[173] *Id.* at 101.

funding of the trusts a fraudulent transfer. *Brooks* is consistent with the bankruptcy court's distain for reactionary avoidance of the bankruptcy trustee and/or lack of candor. Debtors who make full disclosure to the court are rarely denied discharge of indebtedness and may retain assets protected through legitimate planning.

The *Lawrence* case followed *Portnoy* and *Brooks* in 1998.[174] Mr. Lawrence was denied debt discharge, and incarcerated, to coerce repatriation of foreign trust assets. Although Mr. Lawrence clearly funded his trust by fraudulent transfer, fraudulent transfer can be difficult to prove and does not technically invalidate the law governing the foreign trust. The *Lawrence* court (similar to the *Brown* and *Portnoy* rulings) appears to have intentionally avoided reliance on the debtor's fraudulent conveyance. Instead, the court based its holding on the (non-legal) public policy benefits of applying federal and Florida law, as opposed to the law of Mauritius (written into the terms of the Lawrence trust).[175] The court stated:

> This Court is persuaded by the decisions of *Portnoy*, *Brooks* and *Cameron*. The Debtor's rights and obligations under the Mauritian Trust are governed by Florida and federal bankruptcy law, which have an overriding interest in the trust, and not the law of the Republic of Mauritius.[176]

---

[174] *In re Lawrence*, 227 B.R. 907 (Bankr. S.D. Fl. 1998).
[175] *Id.* at 116-18.
[176] *Id.* at 117-18.

The bankruptcy court can therefore be expected to impose "rough justice" on questionable debtors, by attaching (or forcing repatriation of) assets held in a foreign trust. Although the applicable offshore trust law technically protects such assets, the bankruptcy court has made clear its intention to ignore foreign law when the debtor seems undeserving of protections or discharge of indebtedness.[177] To avoid judicial intervention, bankruptcy should be avoided. Offshore trusts should (i) be formed and funded on a "sunny day" long before debt is incurred or expected (to avoid the specter of fraudulent transfer) and (ii) limit the grantor's access to trust assets. If the debtor controls distributions, he or she may face jail time for refusing to repatriate trust assets. Foreign trusts should irrevocably place assets abroad and at the discretion of an offshore trustee who is prohibited from compliance with a U.S. repatriation order.

In conclusion, bankruptcy courts tend to favor creditors in the cat and mouse game between debtors (attempting to hide assets abroad) and creditors (looking for a way to reach the cheese). Unfortunately for the debtor, the bankruptcy court is willing to incarcerate an uncooperative mouse. Moreover, the bankruptcy court may draw on precedent ignoring the law of a debtor friendly jurisdiction to enforce creditor rights based on local law.

---

[177] *In re Brown* (*Higashi v. Brown*), No. 95-3072 (Bankr. D.AK. 1996)(memorandum decision).

Despite the bankruptcy precedent, debtor friendly foreign law and the practice of holding assets abroad remain substantial creditor obstacles. This is especially true regarding jurisdictions offering protective trust and LLC statutes, prohibiting the enforcement of foreign judgments and limiting fraudulent transfer claims.

6.4   Collection Offshore/Non-Bankruptcy Cases

State courts cannot employ a federal bankruptcy trustee to "stand in the shoes" of the debtor. State courts have limited discretion to disregard the governing law chosen by parties to a trust or LLC. Contempt orders for the repatriation of trust assets by a state court are therefore very rare. U.S. creditors suing in state court to collect foreign trust or LLC assets often find themselves without recourse and forced to attempt collection in the foreign jurisdiction.

In *South Orange Grove Owners Associates v. Orange Grove Partners*,[178] a real estate developer sold defectively constructed condominiums between 1988 and 1989. The owners brought suit in 1992 in the Superior Court of California in Los Angeles County.[179] In 1993, the defendant funded an asset protection trust in the Cook Islands. By the time the plaintiffs obtained a California

---

[178] *515 S. Orange Grove Owners Ass'n. v. Orange Grove Partners*, Plaint No. 208/94, (High Ct. Rarotonga, Cook Islands, Civil Division Nov. 6, 1995).

[179] *Id.*

judgment in 1994 (which exceeded $5,000,000) all assets had been moved to the Cook Islands trust.[180]

When the plaintiffs attempted to enforce the California judgment, no domestic assets were available for collection. The plaintiffs sued in the Cook Islands. Specifically, the plaintiffs sought a Mareva injunction to prevent the trustee from again transferring the assets to another debtor friendly country. The plaintiffs also sued the trustee to disgorge assets placed in trust for the purpose of defrauding creditors. The Cook Islands statute of limitations, however, presented a potential obstacle to recovery.[181]

The debtor claimed that the cause of action was time barred because the condo defects "accrued" in 1988 (barring any claim in the Cook Islands after 1990).[182] The

---

[180] *Id.*

[181] *Id.*

[182] Cook Islands International Trusts Act § 13B(3) states: "An international trust settled or established and a disposition to such trust shall for all purposes be deemed not to have been so settled or established, or the property disposed of with intent to defraud a creditor—(a) if settled, established or the disposition takes place after the expiration of two years from the date that creditor's cause of action accrued; or (b) where settled, established or the disposition takes place before the expiration of two years from the date that the creditor's cause of action accrued, that creditor fails to commence in a court of competent jurisdiction proceedings in respect of that creditor's cause of action before the expiration of one that this subsection shall not have effect if, and subject to subsection (5), at the time of settlement, establishment, or disposition, as the case may be, proceedings in respect of that creditor's cause of action against that settlor have already been

Cook Islands Court, however, held that the plaintiffs' cause of action did not accrue until the date of the California judgment in 1994. The ruling allowed the plaintiffs to timely file suit in the Cook Islands prior to 1996 (two years from the date of the California judgment). The case was, however, settled before collection rights were adjudicated.[183]

Predictably, the Cook Islands legislature quickly eliminated the creditor benefit established by the South Orange ruling. In 1996, the Cook Islands' International Trust Act of 1984 was amended to establish that the "date of the cause of action accruing" (not the date of the later offshore judgment) triggers the start of the limitations period.[184] By amending the statute, the Cook Islands

---

commenced in a court of competent jurisdiction." The term "cause of action" is defined in subclause (8) of § 13B as "(a) the date of the cause of action accruing shall be, the date of that action, and if there is more than one act or the omission shall be a continuing one, the date of the first act or the date that the omission shall have first occurred, as the case may be, shall be the date that the cause of action shall have accrued, (b) the term "cause of action" means the earliest cause of action capable of assertion by a creditor against the settlor of an international trust, or as the case may be, against the settlor of property upon an international trust, by which the creditor has established (or may establish) an enforceable claim against that settlor."

[183] Barry Engel, Does Asset Protection Planning Really Work?, *Journal of Asset Protection*, Sept/Oct. 1998 *available at* http://www.engelreiman.com/articles/Journal_of_Asset_Proteciton.html.

[184] International Trust Act (Cook Islands((1984) § 13B(3)(as amended 1985, 1989, 1991, 1995-96, & 1999) at southpactrust.com/img/InTrustAct.pdf.

legislature eliminated the ability of a plaintiff to claim (the later) date of the U.S. judgment as the starting date of the statute of limitations. The limitations period now starts when the wrongdoing occurs (not when the plaintiff later wins a U.S. judgment). The revision makes timely filing in the Cook Islands practically impossible. Consider, for example, the remote likelihood of a timely filed suit (prior to 1990) by the purchaser of a defective condo (purchased in 1988) litigating in California toward a judgment in 1994.

An example of an American court respecting a Cook Islands trust is *Riechers v. Riechers*,[185] discussed at page 118. In *Riechers*, a New York divorce court denied jurisdiction over the husband's foreign asset protection trust. The court refused to tamper with the trust, funded for the "legitimate purposes of protecting family assets" for the benefits of Riechers' family members. The *Riechers* court did, however, retain jurisdiction over Dr. Riechers. As a result, the court included the trust assets as divisible marital property (even though a Cook Islands court would determine the ultimate disposition of such assets).

6.5   Government Claims

Even with a money judgment and clear proof of fraudulent conveyance, assets may not be practically reachable by creditors of limited means. The likelihood that an individual plaintiff will pay the cost of litigation on

---

[185] *Riechers v. Riechers*, 178 Misc. 2d 170 (1998).

the other side of the world is very low. Collection by the government is, however, more difficult to discourage. The government enjoys unlimited finances and broad powers of collection not available to the public. As detailed in Section 5.5, federal and state governments have broad collection powers, especially where criminal sanctions may be imposed on the debtor.

FTC v. Affordable Media (known as the *Anderson*[186] case because the defendants are named Anderson) reflects the government's willingness to expend substantial resources to collect from a foreign trust. Four years after Stephen Lawrence defaulted on payment obligations to Bear Stearns, Michael and Denyse Anderson defrauded thousands of people through a telemarketing scheme. The Andersons transferred money bilked from investors into a Cook Islands asset protection trust. The Andersons initially served as co-trustees and protectors of the trust.

The Federal Trade Commission's complaint against the Andersons prompted the U.S. District Court (trial court) in Nevada to order the Andersons to repatriate the offshore funds.[187] Instead of ordering funds returned to the U.S., the Andersons requested (via fax) their co-trustee to repatriate the money. The co-trustee immediately removed the Andersons as trustees of the trust and refused repatriation. The trust's "anti-duress" clause authorized the co-trustee to remove the Andersons

---

[186] *FTC v. Affordable Media, LLC*, 179 F. 3d 1228 (9th Cir. 1999).
[187] *Id.* at 1233.

upon the happening of an event of "duress."[188] The District Court's order constituted such an event.[189] The foreign trustee therefore properly rejected the Andersons' request made under judicial coercion. As the Andersons no longer controlled the trust, they argued that their compliance with the order to repatriate trust assets was impossible.

Despite their removal as co-trustees, the District Court did not believe that the Andersons lost control of the trust because, as protectors of the trust, they determine whether an event of duress occurred. As a consequence, the District Court imprisoned the Andersons for civil contempt of court. The District Court did not identify the

---

[188] The Anderson trust agreement contained an anti-duress clause which provided that the "trustee hereof shall automatically cease to be a trustee upon the happening of an event of duress within the territory where such trustee is…resident (in the case of an individual) and upon ceasing to be a trustee pursuant to this clause such trustee shall be divested of title to the property of this trust which shall automatically vest in the remaining or continuing trustee (if any) *located in a territory not having an event of duress and the form for administration* of this trust shall not notwithstanding any other provision in this deed to be deemed the place of residence or incorporation (if a corporation) of such continuing trustee." Id. At 12240 quoting Trust Agreement at 17.

[189] *Id.* at 1240, Fn 9, citing Trust Agreement at 3. The Anderson trust agreement defined an event of duress as including "the issuance of any order, decree or judgment of any court or tribunal in any part of the world which in the opinion of the protector will or may directly or indirectly, expropriate, sequester, levy, lien, or in any way control, restrict or prevent the free disposal by a trustee of any monies, investments or property which may from time to time be included in or form part of this trust and any distribution therefrom."

legal basis for repatriation, but stated in its order that the Andersons were to repatriate all assets in foreign countries held by them or in trust for them. The Andersons appealed, claiming that compliance with the repatriation order was impossible.[190] Before the Ninth Circuit Appeals Court had a chance to rule on the civil contempt order, the District Court released the Andersons after nearly six months in jail.[191]

The Ninth Circuit later affirmed the trial court's civil contempt ruling. In affirming, the Ninth Circuit rejected the "impossibility" defense. The Ninth Circuit determined that the impossibility was self-induced, and therefore not a defense to a contempt ruling.[192]

The reason for the District Court's release of the Andersons after six months in jail (even though they had not repatriated any assets) is unclear. One reason may be that the District Court finally accepted the U.S. Supreme Court precedent that the impossibility to comply is a defense to civil contempt. If incarceration does not lead to repatriation (within a reasonable time), the court must release the debtor from jail.

Another possible reason behind the District Court's release of the Andersons is the FTC's failed offshore legal strategy. In November of 1998, the FTC retained legal counsel in the Cook Islands to investigate forcing repatriation of assets. One strategy was to bring a

---

[190] *Id.* at 1233.
[191] *Id.* at Fn 3.
[192] *Id.* at 1239-44.

fraudulent transfer claim in a Cook Islands court. The second was to require the Andersons, as protectors of the trust, to remove the corporate co-trustee and replace it with an FTC-approved trustee. The FTC pursued the second option, and ordered the Andersons, who were still in jail at the time, to execute documents allowing the FTC to become the corporate co-trustee.

The FTC failed in its efforts to replace the corporate co-trustee with its own co-trustee. The Cook Islands High Court ruled that the replacement of the Andersons' corporate co-trustee breached the trust and assessed litigation costs to the FTC.[193] Moreover, the Cook Islands High Court held that the Cook Islands have no jurisdiction to enforce "a penal revenue or other public law of a foreign state." By refusing to rule on the repatriation issue, the court left the FTC with no recourse.[194] The stolen funds therefore remained in trust. Rumor has it that the case was settled for pennies on the dollar.[195]

The *Anderson* and *Lawrence* cases suggest that the "impossibility defense" to contempt cannot be relied on if the inability of the debtor to reach trust assets was

---

[193] *U.S.A. v. A Limited, Plaint No. 57/1999, High Court of Cook Islands Rarotonga (Civil Division)* http://www.assetprotectionbook.com/forum/viewtopic.php?f=8&t=1080.

[194] *Id.* at 1.

[195] "Commission Approval of Settlement Regarding the Collection of Offshore Assets," Federal Trade Commission Office of Public Affairs, December 13, 2002, http://www.ftc.gov/opa/2002/12/fyi0265.shtm.

established by the debtor's self-serving act. A rejected claim of impossibility (to reach trust assets) exposes the debtor to incarceration for contempt (pending repatriation of trust assets). The issue of "self-imposed" impossibility may, however, be avoided by (i) funding a trust prior to any existing or expected creditor claims and (ii) limiting grantor control over trust distributions. Limiting grantor control may be accomplished by leaving discretion over trust distributions with an unrelated trustee and protector. The issue of impossibility then likely becomes irrefutable.

The U.S. Securities and Exchange Commission ("SEC") was also forced to litigate offshore in the 1999 case of *Conway v. Queensway Trustees Limited.*[196] The case involved securities fraud. Suit was filed by a U.S. bankruptcy trustee in Nevis, West Indies, attempting to reach assets transferred to a self-settled Nevis trust. Litigation in the debtor haven illustrates (i) the practical advantage of keeping assets offshore and (ii) the legal obstacles faced by U.S. creditors' attempting collection in the home country.

In 1995, the Southern District Court of New York ruled in favor of the SEC for more than $71,539,620 in fraudulently obtained profit.[197] Immediately after the

---

[196] *Conway v. Queensway Trustees Ltd.*, Civ. Suit No. 16 of 19999, High Court of Justice, Federation of Saint Christopher and Nevis (Nevis Circuit 1999) *see also*, *Conway v. Queensway Trustees Ltd.*, St. Christopher and Nevis Civ. Appl. No. 11 of 19999 (Ct. App. 2000).

[197] *S.E.C. v. First Jersey Sec., Inc.* 890 F. Supp. 1185, 1195, 1213 (S.D. N.Y. 1995).

judgment, the debtor, Mr. Brennan, filed bankruptcy to reorganize under Chapter 11, but failed to disclose his Nevis trust, funded only a year earlier. The bankruptcy trustee sued in Nevis, claiming that the debtor fraudulently "hid away his assets... in a trust fund still within his reach."[198] The court cited the Nevis International Exempt Trust Ordinance of 1994 ("NIETO"), concluding as follows:

> (i) that an international trust shall be valid and enforceable notwithstanding that it may be invalid under the law of the settlor's domicile or residence;[199] (ii) that §47 of NIETO provides that an international trust shall not be declared invalid or affected in any way if the settlor possesses power to revoke the trust, to amend the trust, to benefit from the trust or to remove or appoint trustees or protectors; (iii) that the Fraudulent Conveyances Act of 1571, shall have no application to any international trust nor any transfer into such trust; and (iv) that §28 of NIETO provides that no proceedings regarding the enforcement or recognition of a foreign judgment against a settlor shall be entertained.[200]

---

[198] *Conway v. Queensway Trustees Ltd., St. Christopher and Nevis Civ. App.* No. 11 of 1999 (Ct. App. 2000).

[199] *Id.* at 8.

[200] *Conway v. Queensway Trustees Ltd., St. Christopher and Nevis Civ. App.* No. 11 of 1999 (Ct. App. 2000).

The Nevis court dismissed the claims, noting that Nevis trusts "may be conducted without too much bother from overly ambitious or malicious detractions." Although Mr. Brennan still faced U.S. prosecutors, the Nevis ruling supports the efficacy of foreign planning.

The most effective way to insure enforcement of protective law (written into an asset protection plan) is to avoid (i) funding the plan with the intention of hiding assets, (ii) retaining absolute control over trust assets, (iii) failing to carefully preserve the legal formalities of any trust or business entity and (iv) becoming subject to bankruptcy or government claims. Proper consideration of the choice of law issue requires professional guidance.

Chapter 7: Business Structures

*"[T]he majority today steps across the line of statutory
interpretation and reaches far into the realm of rewriting
this legislative act." – Florida Supreme Court Justice Fred
Lewis (2010)*[201]

7.1   Corporations and "Inside" Asset Protection

7.1.1   Corporations in General

Business entities have existed for centuries to
legally separate the obligations of a legal person ("corp")
from its owner. The corporation is a legal fiction that may

---

[201] *Olmstead v. F.T.C.*, 44 So. 2d 76, 83 (2010) (J. Lewis) (dissent).

147

engage in business and incur debts separate and apart from its owners and operators. The corporation has developed as the most common business entity in the U.S. and is generally characterized by its issuance of "shares" of capital or equity.

Corporate shares represent investment in the entity and the limit of investor risk. Shares may be voting or nonvoting and may be issued with preferred dividends or other shareholder preferences. Corporations are governed by a board of directors appointed by its shareholders. The board appoints officers (employees of the corporation) to manage daily business operations. Corporations include all U.S. state entities with the suffix "inc.," "incorporated," "corp.," "corporation," "P.A." or "P.C." (professional corporation).

The asset protection feature associated with corporations is the insulation of shareholders from the obligations of the entity. Corporations enable owners to control business operations of the corporation without personal exposure to "inside" business debts. This protection is referred to as "inside" asset protection. It is also commonly referred to as "inside-out" protection because a creditor "inside" the business of the corporation cannot get "out" to the assets of the owner.

Inside protection eliminates the risks associated with operating as a sole proprietor. A sole proprietorship is created when a single individual starts a business without any additional formality. Although the sole proprietorship is the most common form of business, it is a very risky arrangement because the individual owner is liable for all debts of the business. The sole proprietorship should be avoided.

Corporate legal formalities must be carefully followed and reflected in written director and shareholder minutes. Corporate finances must be treated as separate from that of the owners. Without legal and financial separation of the corporation from the personal activities of its owners, the corporation may be ignored as an "alter ego" of its owners, leaving the shareholders liable for debts of the entity. If the debtor fails to respect the distinctions between entity and owner (such as separate books, accounts, expenditures and governance), a judge may disregard any inside asset protection. Rulings allowing a business creditor to "pierce the corporate veil" are uncommon but the case law varies from state to state.

Professionals, such as doctors and lawyers, cannot fully benefit from corporate "inside" asset protection. Professionals are personally responsible for their own negligence (even if services are provided through a corporation). Professional corporations insulate the professional owner only from business liabilities unrelated to services, such as supply contracts and lease obligations. Professionals are treated as sole proprietors regarding malpractice claims.

Shares in corporations are not protected. A creditor of a shareholder may attach the debtor's shares to satisfy a judgment. In other words, publicly traded stock in IBM and shares in a small corporation will both be lost (along with other unprotected assets) in a collection action against the shareholder. The judgment creditor will become a shareholder, with all associated voting, dividend, accounting and liquidation rights.[202]

The action is known as "reverse veil piercing." The name comes from the traditional business creditor remedy of "piercing the corporate veil," i.e., breaking through the entity to the "outside" assets of the owner. Traditional "veil piercing" from inside a business entity, to reach the personal assets of the business owner, is reversed when a personal creditor of the owner seeks assets in the owner's business entity.

Shareholders can establish a somewhat imperfect means of preventing the transfer of shares to a shareholder's creditor. To this end, the shareholders may contractually establish the right of the corporation and/or other shareholders to purchase shares exposed to a creditor. Such purchase options, if exercised, prevent the creditor from obtaining equity in the corporation. "Cross-purchase" or redemption strategies are, however, often cumbersome because the purchaser(s) must pay for shares under potentially undesirable economic circumstances. They also require the existence of more than one shareholder.

---

[202] *Cf.* NV Stat. 78.746, limiting creditors of shareholders in Nevada corporations to a charging order on such shares, provided that the Nevada corporation is not publicly traded, has less than 100 shareholders and is not a professional corporation. *See* Section 7.2 regarding charging order protection.

Stock purchase options are necessary due to the U.S. states having adopted the English historical mandate that corporate stock be "alienable." In other words, shareholders cannot contractually prohibit stock transfers (whether voluntary or involuntary). Shareholders comply with such "rule against inalienability" by establishing purchase options allowing the corporation and remaining shareholders to circumvent a transfer to an outside party. "Shareholders agreements" also typically include the right to purchase shares held by a deceased or disabled shareholder.

The corporate philosophy behind buyout triggers is to avoid equity transfers to outside parties. A similar philosophy supports the purchase of shares held by shareholders no longer working for the corporation. When an owner stops working, he or she is often treated like an outsider (subject to buy-out). "Shareholders Agreements" and "Buy-Sell Contracts" are defensive measures against undesirable equity transfers and unproductive shareholder/employees.

Shareholders sued on matters unrelated to corporate business must surrender corporate stock to the creditor or accept the buyout terms of any applicable shareholders agreement. Any cash payment for shares becomes available to the judgment holder. As the number of shareholders increases, the likelihood of shareholder collection litigation (exposing corporate stock) increases.

Unlike partnerships, corporations are taxed independently on profits. Profits are taxed again when distributed as dividends to shareholders. If, however, a U.S. corporation is owned by not more than one hundred individuals (all of whom are U.S. residents or citizens), the corporation may avoid tax at the corporate level. This is achieved by making the "S" election, under Subchapter S of the Internal Revenue Code. "S" corporations are not taxed and profits are "passed through" to the shareholders for tax purposes. "S" corporations are therefore typically more tax efficient than (the alternative) "C" corporations.

Despite the obvious benefits, "S" corporations are often less flexible than partnerships (discussed starting on page 156) from a tax perspective. "S" corporations are restrictive because they often tax property distributions to owners and must allocate taxable profit and losses precisely in accordance with ownership percentages. Also, if an owner is not a U.S. citizen or resident or if the owners exceed one hundred in number, the "S" election is not available. In such cases, partnership tax status (or, in the case of a single member LLC, "disregarded" tax status) is the only permissible "pass through" format. "S" corporations may, however, be more tax efficient for active service or manufacturing businesses which employ the owner(s). Choosing a tax status requires the weighing of various factors by a seasoned professional.

7.1.2   Foreign Corporations

Corporations are available in many offshore jurisdictions. Although foreign corporations are similar to those offered by each of the fifty states, the structure of offshore entities is determined by a foreign government.

Also, U.S. courts have no jurisdiction over a foreign corporation not doing business in the U.S.

In light of the often cumbersome requirements of foreign corporate organizational statutes, and the advent of the more streamlined offshore LLC, the usefulness of the foreign corporation has waned. Nonetheless, the confidentiality associated with certain offshore corporations may be attractive. Depending on the governing law, offshore corporate officers and directors may ignore U.S. claims and are difficult to depose. Several foreign jurisdictions have implemented confidentiality statutes and anti-domestication laws. Such laws require offshore officers and directors to refrain from releasing corporate information.

Several debtor friendly jurisdictions also offer the so-called "international business corporation" (IBC) to foreigners. The IBC is typically not taxed by the home country and allows for the use of corporate "nominees." Only the "nominees" chosen by the owners are reflected on the public record of the organizing jurisdiction.

Offshore corporations therefore provide confidentiality and a certain level of asset protection. However, they generally fail to match the protections offered by the foreign charging order entities (discussed below) and usually involve complex board and nominee requirements. Also, the foreign corporation does not offer the simplicity of direct owner management or disregarded tax treatment. Foreign corporations must be taxed as "C" corporations, and may not make the "S" election (to avoid double taxation of corporate profits and shareholder dividends).

7.2 Charging Order Protected Entities and "Outside" Asset Protection

All fifty states and several foreign jurisdictions offer partnerships and limited liability companies. LLCs and partnerships provide "outside" asset protection. Unlike corporate stock, which may be attached by any creditor of a shareholder, equity held in a protective partnership or LLC cannot be reached by a creditor of an owner. An "outside" creditor (of a member or partner) cannot acquire a voting interest or any assets of a protective LLC or partnership. However, the strength of the applicable organizational statute will determine the degree of outside protection.

Creditors of partners or LLC members are limited to placing a "charging order" on the equity of the debtor/partner. Partnerships and LLCs are therefore known as "charging order entities." The charging order lien entitles the creditor only to company distributions (if any) payable to the debtor, but not to any liquidation, voting or management authority. The holder of a charging order cannot sell the debtor's ownership interest, force distribution of company assets or vote on any company matters. The limitation on an "outside" creditor to a charging order is what creates "outside asset protection." Such outside protection of equity is also referred to as "outside-in" protection because the "outside" creditor of an owner cannot get "in" to the assets of the partnership or LLC. Chart 7.2 illustrates the charging order concept.

Chart 7.2

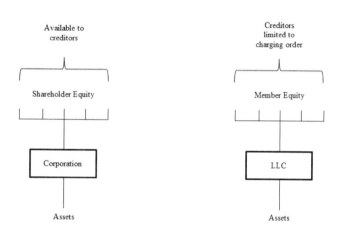

The Charging Order

There are two principal advantages of outside asset protection: First, it eliminates the instability associated with involuntary transfers of voting rights (which plagues corporations). Second, individual members/partners benefit from the "outside" creditor protection of their equity. If the debtor holds equity in a publicly traded, separately managed or otherwise widely held LLC or limited partnership, the charging lien may provide sufficient distributions to motivate collection on a judgment. However, if the debtor's interest is in a closely held company, management may decide to withhold exposed distributions. A general partner or managing member supportive of the debtor will, of course, refrain from distributions benefitting the creditor. Powerless to force collection, the creditor will typically accept a marginal settlement (to release the charging order).

If properly funded and organized in a debtor friendly jurisdiction, charging order entities substantially reduce the creditor exposure associated with corporate shares. Collection on a charged LLC or partnership interest is cumbersome and expensive. The creditor usually has little interest in waiting for discretionary distributions to the debtor or being potentially saddled with the tax liability associated with undistributed profits. Debtors considering bankruptcy should, however, keep in mind that bankruptcy law conditions charging order protection on the debtor being required for management or other company obligations. If the debtor is "non-executory" (i.e., completely passive), the bankruptcy trustee may make the debtor's equity available to creditors.

7.2.1   Partnerships

Historically, the alternative to the corporation has been the partnership. A partnership is an association between two or more people engaged in a business venture for profit. Partnerships may take the form of a general partnership or a limited partnership.

A general partnership is owned and controlled by the partners, all of which are general partners. There is no separation of ownership and management. General partners are jointly and severally (individually) liable for all debts of the partnership. This arrangement is usually unintended and saddles each partner with all partnership debts and all liabilities arising from the business acts of all partners. The general partnership is actually the only business format less desirable than the sole proprietorship (an individual operating without any business formality or protection). Under no circumstances should any venture take the form of a general partnership.

The limited partnership, on the other hand, allows for so called "limited partners," along with at least one general partner. The general partners are in control of the partnership and liable for all partnership obligations. Limited partners have no managerial authority or liquidation rights. Limited partners are protected by inside asset protection and risk only their investment to creditors of the limited partnership. A creditor of the limited partnership cannot reach the personal assets of a limited partner. The general partner remains liable for all partnership obligations.

Before LLCs, limited partnerships were the entity of choice to capitalize passive investment. As an example, a real estate developer or entrepreneur in need of capital could sell limited partnership interests without jeopardizing his controlling position. The limited partnership provides a means of capitalizing a project (by selling limited partner interests), without exposing the founder to a loss of majority control.

The origins of the limited partnership are centuries old. It existed in France in the Middle Ages as "La Société en Commandite."[203] The statutes of the city-states of Pisa and Florence recognize it as far back as the year 1160. In the Middle Ages, it was one of the most frequent entities of trade and the legal foundation for investment in Mediterranean maritime commerce.[204] The limited partnership even travelled under the protection of the Crusaders to the City of Jerusalem.[205]

During the Middle Ages, capital was concentrated in the hands of nobles and clergy, who, due to caste or canonical regulations, could not engage directly in trade. The limited partnership allowed for secret participation by a "silent" partner, without personal risk. Such secrecy and limited exposure provided a means for investment and the economic exploitation of vast wealth. Thus, the otherwise idle wealth of the aristocracy and clergy "became the foundation, by means of this ingenious idea, of great commerce which made princes of the merchants, elevated the trading classes, and brought the commons into position as an influential estate in the commonwealth."[206]

In the United States, limited partnerships have existed since New York State's adoption of the first limited partnership statute in 1822. The origin, history and

---

[203] David Shepard Garland, John Houston Merrill, Thomas Johnson Michie, Charles Frederic Williams eds., The American and English Encyclopedia of Law Vol. 13, 804 (Edward Thompson Company Law Pub.) (1890).

[204] Henry Hansmann, Reinier Kraakman, and Richard Squire, *Law and the Rise of the Firm*, 119 Harv. L. Rev. 1333, 1364-1374 (2006).

[205] *Ames v. Downing*, 1 Bradf. 321, 329-30 (1850).

[206] *Id.*

purpose of the limited partnership were described by a New York court in *Ames v. Downing* (1850). The Ames court described the limited partnership as "introduced by statute into this State, and subsequently very generally adopted in many other States of the Union ... [and] borrowed from the French Code."[207]

Limited partnerships are not inadvertently formed (like sole proprietorships or general partnerships). Every U.S. state has a limited partnership act. Each act requires registration and the designation of a registered agent (in such state) to accept service of a lawsuit.

The inherent drawback to the limited partnership is the unlimited liability of the general partner ("GP") for debts of the entity. To address the issue, corporations were used for decades to hold the exposed general partnership interest. The person in charge would own the general partner interest through a corporation, to establish an "inside" liability shield from partnership obligations. The equity held by the corporate GP, however, remained exposed to "inside" partnership creditors (and to outside creditors of the individual shareholder). To limit the exposure, the corporate GP would own only a minor percentage of the limited partnership. The investors (which may include the owner of the GP) would then hold the remainder of the equity as limited partners. Although this arrangement functions to limit general partner liability, it can be cumbersome. The structure is also

---

[207] *Id.; see also* William George, The Handbook of the Law of Partnership, §§ 184-5, 419 West Publishing (1897).

exposed to the involuntary transfer of stock in the corporate GP. Any creditor of the owner of the GP may attach the GP stock and take control of the partnership.

Considering the unlimited liability of general partners (for the debts of the partnership), modern business entities are seldom organized as general partnerships. Even limited partnerships (which require a general partner) have become less common. Almost all states have adopted limited liability partnership ("LLP") statutes, to limit general partner liability in general partnerships.[208] Ten states have enacted similar legislation, to limit GP liability associated with limited partnerships.[209] Limited liability limited partnerships are known as LLLPs. The partnership makes a simple filing to add the limited liability "LL" to the P (general partnership) or LP (limited partnership). Electing LLP or LLLP status insulates the general partner(s) from liabilities of the partnership. Although the degree of protection varies from state to state, the filing has no adverse implications. It should therefore be considered for existing partnerships.

Almost all U.S. states have also enacted statutes allowing for the conversion of partnerships to a more protective entity. Existing limited and general partnerships should take advantage of the legislation and

---

[208] Uniform Partnership Act (1997) Addendum to Prefatory Note, Nat'l Conference of Commissioners on Uniform State Laws, July 12-19 1996.

[209] "Limited Liability Limited Partnership" Wikipedia, http//en.wikipedia.org/wiki/Limited_liability_limited_partnership, accessed January 29, 2012.

consider converting to limited liability company status. Business obligations incurred after conversion are obligations solely of the LLC (not its owners).

7.2.2   The Limited Liability Company

The limited liability company ("LLC") is relatively recent to the U.S. Similar entities have, however, operated in other countries for centuries. The first American LLC statute was adopted by Wyoming in 1977. Every state has since instituted the LLC.

The LLC combines (i) corporate inside protection (from business debts) with (ii) partnership outside protection (from creditors of owners). LLCs are formed as entities separate from their owners by filing Articles of Organization. If established in a favorable jurisdiction, LLCs offer the benefits of both corporations and partnerships. LLCs must reflect the suffix "LLC," "LC," "limited liability company," "limited company," "chartered" or "PL" (professional LLC), depending on the state (or country) of organization.

LLCs are very flexible in terms of corporate governance. There is no requirement for a "board of directors" or officers, such as a president and treasurer. The LLC may be governed directly by the owners (known as "members"), acting by majority, unanimity or otherwise. One member could, alternatively, be appointed "managing member" (similar to a general partner), with no personal liability. Another option is the appointment of an unrelated "manager" or a "board of managers," with partial or complete managerial control over the LLC. The "managing members" or, if independent, the "managers" are not liable for the debts of the LLC.

Note that such managerial flexibility allows for organizational errors not typically possible under the more rigid corporate statutes. For example, many state corporate statutes set standards for the content of Articles of Incorporation and Bylaws. Even agreements among shareholders must often comply with statutory guidelines. The various LLC statutes, on the other hand, almost universally authorize the members to create their own managerial rules through an operating agreement. In light of the potential for error, an experienced attorney should always be utilized to ensure that LLC governance documents are properly prepared.

Tax Status of LLCs

The IRS affords the LLC substantial flexibility in its choice of tax status. The LLC may elect the tax attributes of (i) a corporation (either "S" or "C"), (ii) a disregarded entity (if owned by a single member) or (iii) a partnership (if owned by more than one taxpayer). These are distinct categories of U.S. taxation, each of which was previously applicable only to a specific type of business entity. Unlike the other entities, the LLC may choose from a variety of tax categories. For domestic LLCs, the IRS requires the election of a tax status only if corporate status is desired. Otherwise, the LLC will be treated as disregarded (if held by a single member) or as a tax partnership (if held by multiple members). Although this book provides only a flavor for the tax treatment of LLCs, it should be understood that the flexibility of LLC tax status and governance allows for almost unlimited business use of the LLC.

The "S" tax format (named from "Subchapter S" of the Internal Revenue Code) is typically the most efficient for active businesses (as opposed to passive investment). This is the case because some profits may potentially be distributed to owner/employees without the added cost of self-employment tax. However, "S" tax status is less flexible than partnership or disregarded tax status. Passive investment ventures should typically avoid "S" status because of potential tax on property transfers to owners and restrictions on distributions not proportionate to ownership percentages. Real estate investment companies involved in a variety of transactions usually benefit most from partnership or disregarded tax status.

The single owner LLC (disregarded for tax purposes) has created novel tax planning opportunities. In particular, the disregarded LLC allows the owner to take advantage of LLC "inside" protections while avoiding tax filings for the entity. In other words, an LLC may be used to isolate business or investment liabilities without the need for an additional tax return. A business arrangement requiring multiple related entities may also be completely disregarded for tax purposes. If organized properly, a conglomerate of LLCs (owned entirely by the founder) requires only a personal tax return.

Take, for example, the single real estate investor with three rental houses. Before the LLC, the single owner was generally forced to create an "S" corporation which would own subsidiary "S" corporations. Each subsidiary would hold a single property, to insulate the other subsidiaries from liabilities of each property (such as a slip and fall). The structure (outlined in Chart 7.2.2-A) creates inside liability protection. However, the "S" corp. holding company remains exposed to creditors of its owner (which, in turn, exposes the entire structure). The structure therefore lacks outside asset protection.

Chart 7.2.2–A

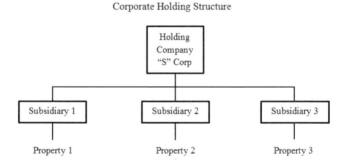

Corporate Holding Structure

The "S" corporation structure also requires the filing of (i) IRS Form 2553 (to establish "S" corporation status of the holding company), (ii) IRS Form 1120S (annual "S" return), (iii) IRS Form 8869 (to establish each "S" subsidiary) and (iv) IRS Form 1122 (annually for each subsidiary).

A similar real estate holding company structure may now be implemented using LLCs. An LLC holding company may own LLC subsidiaries (disregarded for tax purposes), each holding an insulated rental property. A "disregarded" entity is protective for state law purposes, but ignored (as distinct from its owner) for tax purposes. No tax return is required for disregarded entities. The subsidiary LLCs provide inside asset protection against business and investment liabilities arising in each subsidiary (similar to the corporate structure). The difference, from a tax perspective, is that all of the LLCs are disregarded (eliminating the need for any tax returns) and avoid the cumbersome "S" corporation restrictions.

Unfortunately, the judicial trend is to invalidate outside asset protection of LLCs held by a single owner. The single member holding company LLC could therefore create exposure. If possible, a second member should be added to the holding company. The addition of a member usually has no tax impact, but necessitates a partnership tax return (Form 1065). The subsidiaries remain disregarded for tax purposes and do not file separate tax returns. A popular structure for a family holding company LLC is illustrated in Chart 7.2.2-B.

An additional disregarded subsidiary can be organized to manage the back-office operation of the active subsidiaries. The management LLC assumes substantial operational liability (by contracting with the other subsidiaries) yet holds no assets. The management company absorbs operational and employee liability of the

Asset Protection

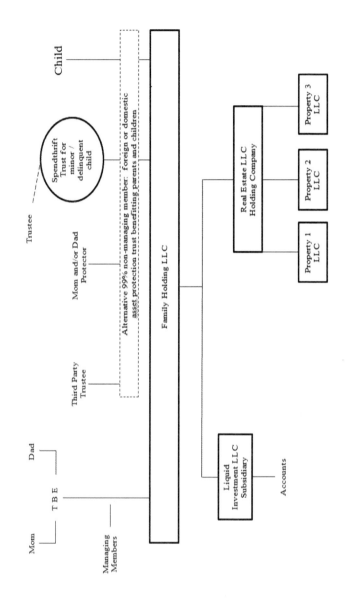

Chart 7.2.2-B

Mom ⎤
    ⎥ T B E
Dad ⎦

Managing Members

Third Party Trustee

Mom and/or Dad Protector

Trustee

Child

Spendthrift Trust for minor / delinquent child

Alternative 99% non-managing member: foreign or domestic asset protection trust benefitting parents and children

Family Holding LLC

Liquid Investment LLC Subsidiary

Accounts

Real Estate LLC Holding Company

Property 1 LLC

Property 2 LLC

Property 3 LLC

active subsidiaries and allows for a consolidated operation (with a single bank account and centralized accounting).

The LLC conglomerate insulates the owners from business and investment exposures and (if properly formed) shields subsidiary assets from creditors. An additional advantage is that fractional interests in the holding company can sometimes be utilized for tax discounted gifts (to shift wealth to the next generation).

Single Member LLCs

In recent years, the charging order protection of the single member LLC has deteriorated. Several states provide statutory creditor protection to multi-member and single member LLCs. Such protection generally limits creditors seeking LLC equity to a "charging order." The charging order remedy limits creditors to LLC distributions. The creditor may not attach voting rights or force liquidation of the LLC. Unfortunately the statutory protections applicable to single member LLCs have been weakened, both in the bankruptcy context and regarding the Florida LLC.

The 2003 Colorado bankruptcy case of *In re Albright* reflects the power of the bankruptcy court to ignore applicable law (in this case, the Colorado LLC statute), to protect a creditor.[210] The court held that when the single member of an LLC files for bankruptcy, charging order protection is not available to protect the

---

[210] *In re Albright*, 291 B.R. 538 (Bankr. D. Co. 2003).

debtor's LLC interest.[211]   The Albright court established the precedent that charging order protection is not available to a bankrupt owner of a single member LLC.

The Albright court allowed the bankruptcy trustee to transfer the LLC interest of the single bankrupt member to his creditors. The creditors could in turn liquidate the LLC (i.e., sell LLC assets) to pay the debts of the member. The Bankruptcy Court based its decision to disregard state statutory protections on a historical partnership principle. The court determined that the charging order was historically established to protect the partnership and partners other than the debtor.   In other words, the partnership charging order (predecessor to the LLC) was implemented to shield the other non-debtor partners. According to the court, the historical basis for the protection does not apply to an entity owned by one person.[212]   In so ruling, the court negated Colorado's charging order protection over solo LLCs in the bankruptcy context (even though the applicable state statue entitles all Colorado LLCs to charging order protection).

The bankruptcy court later confirmed its position taken in Albright.   In the 2006 case of *In re A-Z Electronics, LLC*, an Idaho bankruptcy court ruled that the bankruptcy trustee "steps into the shoes" of the debtor/solo LLC member.[213]   The trustee can exercise all LLC managerial powers of the debtor/member.[214]   In the 2007

---

[211] *Id.* at 542.

[212] *In re Albright*, 291 B.R. 538 (Bankr. D. Co. 2003).

[213] *In re A-Z Electronics, LLC*, 350 B.R. 886 (Bankr. D. Idaho 2006).

[214] *Id.*

case of *In re Modanlo*, a Maryland bankruptcy court authorized the bankruptcy trustee (of a solo member's estate) to continue business operations of the LLC (even after LLC dissolution caused by the member's bankruptcy).[215] The court permitted the trustee to designate itself as manager of the LLC.[216]

Outside the bankruptcy setting, the Florida Supreme Court invalidated the language in the revised Florida Statutes protecting single member LLCs. The case involved a Federal Trade Commission judgment against defendants Shawn Olmstead and Julie Connell. The FTC sought assets held in single member LLCs, as part of a collection action to recover more than $10,000,000 in restitution for victims of the defendants' credit card scam. The Florida Supreme Court ruled that a debtor may be forced to surrender equity in a single member LLC to satisfy an outstanding judgment.

Similar to the bankruptcy court in Albright, the Florida Supreme Court disregarded the Florida statutory language protecting all Florida LLCs. The *Olmstead* Court did so by analogizing LLC equity to freely transferable (exposed) corporate stock.[217] The Court further supported the unraveling of the single member LLC by citing the omission by the Florida legislature of the word "exclusive" in its statutory language.[218] In the absence of statutory language specifically limiting

---

[215] *In re Modanlo*, 412 B.R. 715 (Bankr. D. Md. 2006).
[216] *Id.*
[217] *Olmstead v. FTC*, 44 So. 3d 76 (Fl. 2010).
[218] *Id.* at 82.

creditors "exclusively" to a charging order, the Court took the liberty of ignoring the difference between corporations and LLCs.[219] The case is yet another example of legislation by judicial edict, to expose assets of a bad actor. Although well intended, the case will eliminate legitimate planning opportunities and force existing single member Florida LLC owners to seek a more protective entity.[220]

Soon after the Olmstead decision, the Florida legislature passed a bill adding the necessary "exclusivity" language to the Florida LLC statute. Any creditor of a member is now limited "exclusively" to a charging order on the debtor's Florida LLC interest.[221] The revised statute, however, allows the creditor to foreclose any membership interest held in a single member Florida LLC. To reach the solo membership interest, the creditor must prove that LLC distributions (to the creditor with a charging order) will not satisfy the judgment within a reasonable time. The law provides no guidance as to the meaning of "reasonable time" or what constitutes a second member. The Florida courts must therefore determine (i) the extent to which parties related to an LLC founder will be treated as a second member (to avoid single member status) and (ii) the standard for distributions necessary to protect the single member Florida LLC.

---

[219] *Id.*

[220] *See* Nev. Stat. § 86.401; Wy. Stat. § 17-29-503 (specifically limiting creditors of a single member to a charging order).

[221] Fl. Stat. § 608.433.

Although the *Olmstead* ruling and resulting legislation will likely eliminate any advantage of the Florida single member LLC over the corporation, the single member LLC may remain protected (outside of bankruptcy court) in states which have adopted more precise legislation. The laws of Nevada and Wyoming specifically limit the creditor of an LLC member to a charging order, even if the LLC is held by a single member.

Single member LLCs formed in less protective states (such as Florida and Colorado) should be converted to a more protective LLC and (if possible) a second member should be added. If a distinct second owner is not an option, issuing ownership to one or several trusts (controlled by the same or related individuals) may suffice. The structure may even be disregarded for tax purposes if ultimately controlled by the founding individual.

Conversion from Corporation to LLC

Owners of closely held corporations should consider converting the corporation to a limited liability company (taxed as a corporation). Conversion will protect LLC equity and shield business and investment assets from shareholder creditors. Converting to a protective LLC will avoid the risk of business disruption and loss of equity associated with an action against a shareholder.

Many jurisdictions accommodate the conversion from corporate to LLC (or partnership) status. The conversion may take the form of a statutory change or merger by the corporation into an LLC. The states allowing conversion are: Alabama, Alaska, Arkansas, California, Colorado, Delaware, Florida, Georgia, Hawaii, Idaho, Illinois, Indiana, Iowa, Kansas, Kentucky, Louisiana, Maine, Maryland, Massachusetts, Michigan, Minnesota, Nebraska, Nevada, New Hampshire, New Jersey, New Mexico, North Carolina, North Dakota, Ohio, Oklahoma, Oregon, Pennsylvania, Rhode Island, South Carolina, Tennessee, Texas and Utah.

Interestingly, if the shareholders do not agree to a conversion, a prudent stockholder can contribute his or her equity to a wholly owned LLC, disregarded for tax purposes. The contribution will not violate the "S" corporation tax restrictions. However, the LLC jurisdiction must be carefully chosen, as the development of the law in some states (regarding the single member LLC) may undermine the protections desired.

The IRS has allowed the tax neutral conversion of an "S" corporation to an LLC. The resulting LLC must, however, qualify as an "S" corporation. "S" corporation shares may only be held by U.S. citizens or residents (up to 100) or by a single entity taxed as an "S" corporation. The types of conversions the IRS has permitted include the transfer of "S" corporation assets to a new LLC, the merger of an "S" corporation into an LLC and the statutory conversion of an "S" corporation to an LLC.

Failing to properly establish the tax status of the LLC converted from a corporation could have devastating tax consequences. The merger or conversion of an existing corporation to an LLC (taxed as a partnership) triggers the liquidation of the corporation for tax purposes and the deemed sale of its assets to its owners. Any taxable gain triggered by the deemed sale creates an immediate tax liability. Any proposed conversion should therefore be carefully reviewed by a tax professional.

The Right Entity for the Job

In light of the LLC's dual protection ("inside" insulation from business liabilities and "outside" charging order equity protection), why use anything else? There is actually no reason to use a corporation or partnership for anything (except certain large securities transactions). The combined protection makes corporations archaic and eliminates the issue of exposed general partners. The question therefore is not whether to use the LLC, but which LLC to use.

LLCs differ from state to state and from country to country. The goal is to find the most protective entity for the proposed business or investment arrangement. To understand the differences between LLCs, one must understand the origins of the LLC law adopted by the states. The historical legal framework emanates from the uniform acts originally proposed to the states. The uniform acts are proposed to the state legislatures by the National Conference of Commissioners on Uniform State Laws.[222] The acts are intended to create consistent and

---

[222] The National Conference of Commissioners on Uniform State Laws (also known as the Uniform Law Commission (ULC)) was established in 1892, and provides states with non-partisan guidance

coherent uniformity among the states. Unfortunately, state LLC law has developed sporadically from a patchwork of uniform acts and cases.

Several "uniform" acts have been drafted over the last century to provide a suggested format for the codification of state partnership and LLC law. The principal uniform acts are (i) the 1914 and 1997 Uniform Partnership Acts (collectively, "UPA"), (ii) the Uniform Limited Partnership Act of 1916 ("ULPA"), (iii) the Revised Uniform Limited Partnership Act ("RULPA") of 1976 and (iv) the Uniform Limited Liability Company Act ("ULLCA") of 1995. The charging order concept is included in each Act. The strength of the protection offered by each Act, however, varies dramatically.

The charging order concept was first proposed for partnerships in the UPA. From its inception, the charging order insulated each partner from creditors of other partners. Many states adopted (some or all of) the UPA to restrict creditors of a partner to a lien on distributions payable to the debtor partner. The lien on distributions would remain in place until its expiration or until the debt (secured by the lien) was paid. UPA established the first protection of partnership equity, to shield non-debtor partners from the personal debts of the other owners.

Unfortunately, the charging order language of UPA (both the 1914 and 1997 acts), ULPA (regarding limited

---

to critical areas of state statutory law. More information at www.nccusl.org/Narrative.aspx?title=About%20the%20ULC

partnerships) and ULLCA (regarding LLCs), does not limit the creditor to distributions otherwise payable to the debtor/owner. The applicable provisions actually authorize the creditor to foreclose partnership/LLC economic interests subject to a charging order. Under such Acts, a charging order constitutes a lien on the debtor's distributional interest, which may be foreclosed at any time. The purchaser at the foreclosure sale permanently obtains the rights of the debtor to distributions. The purchaser will receive all distributions associated with the foreclosed interest, whether made from available cash (from operations) or upon dissolution.

The Georgia LLC statute, for example, is based on the UPA of 1914 and provides that the charging order is not an exclusive remedy.[223] The implication is that the creditor may seek a court order to foreclose (and sell) the LLC distributional interest. Once the interest is foreclosed, the amount of distributions made to the creditor are not limited to the unpaid debt.

Several courts have confirmed that the ULLCA language also allows a creditor of an LLC member to foreclose the distributional interest of the debtor. The creditor acquires the right to profit distributions which may be foreclosed and sold. The difference between a charging order lien and a distributional interest received in foreclosure is that the charging order represents only a lien (until the debt is paid), not a levy, on the debtor's

---

[223] Official Code of Georgia Annotated, "O.C.G.A." § 14-11-504 (a)(b) (2011).

economic interest. The "distributional interest" received by foreclosing a charging order transfers ownership of the economic interest to the creditor. In either case, the creditor holds only an economic interest, not any managerial or voting interests.

However, the real exposure is not the creditor's right to foreclose a charging lien. The exposure comes from the judicial propensity (fueled by the creditor's foreclosure right) to completely disregard any limitation on creditor remedies. In such cases, the judge allows attachment of the debtor's membership interest, exposing LLC managerial control and assets. As discussed starting on page 167, this has happened in Colorado, Idaho, Maryland and Florida, regarding single member LLCs.

The right to foreclose ULLCA LLC interests creates a trap for unaware residents of states with compromised LLC statutes. The use of a ULLCA based LLC (not limiting the creditor exclusively to a charging order) is ill-advised. Superior charging order protection is available in other states (and countries). To make matters worse, a creditor with an ULLCA charging order may seek a judicial determination that the LLC should be dissolved.[224] The states and commonwealths which have adopted ULLCA are as follows: Alabama, Hawaii, Illinois, Montana, South Carolina, South Dakota, Vermont, and West Virginia and the Virgin Islands.

---

[224] Uniform Limited Liability Act (1996) § 503(e)(3), drafted by the National Conference of Commissioners on Uniform State Loans.

RULPA, on the other hand, limits the creditor to partnership distributions otherwise payable to the debtor partner.[225] A 1976 RULPA style charging order does not (at least at the time this book was published) lead to the foreclosure or sale of the debtor partner's interest.[226] The idea is that partnership assets are owned by the entity, rather than by any individual partners or members. The creditor is rendered powerless to impact the operation of the partnership. The following states have further refined the 1976 RULPA (regarding limited partnerships) to clarify that the partnership charging order is the exclusive remedy available to creditors of RULPA partners: Alaska, Arizona, Florida, Nevada, Oklahoma, South Dakota and Texas. Alaska, Florida, South Dakota and Texas have even included language specifically prohibiting other remedies, such as foreclosure.

LLCs which limit creditors exclusively to a charging order are similarly insulated from foreclosure of member equity. The LLC organizational statute chosen should exclusively preclude collection rights beyond a

---

[225] Revised Uniform Limited Partnership Act ("RULPA") (1976) § 703 drafted by the National Conference of Commissioners on Uniform State Laws ; *see also* the RULPA of 2001, allowing for foreclosures but adopted by only Arkansas, California, Hawaii, Idaho, Illinois, Iowa, Louisiana, Maine, Minnesota, New Mexico, North Dakota and Washington. *Available at* http://www.law.upenn.edu/bll/ archives/ulc/ulpa/final2001.htm.

[226] *Cf. In re Allen*, 228 B.R. 115, 120 (Bankr. W.D. Pa. 1998) (a charging order is not the sole remedy available to a creditor of a RULPA partner), *Nigri v. Lotz*, 453 S.E. 2d 780, 782-82 (Ga. App. 1995) (A partner's interest in a RULPA limited partnership can be foreclosed), regarding the 2001 RULPA.

charging order. Several states have implemented protective LLC charging order provisions. Such states include Arizona, Arkansas, Connecticut, Delaware, District of Columbia, Florida (for multi-member LLCs), Idaho, Illinois, Kentucky, Louisiana, Maryland, Minnesota, Mississippi, Nevada, Oklahoma, Rhode Island, Texas, Virginia and Wyoming.

Interestingly, Florida adopted exclusivity language for its limited partnership but failed to use protective charging order language in its LLC statute (until recently revised to protect multi-member LLCs). The prior Florida LLC statute was dismantled by the Florida Supreme Court in 2010, to expose equity in the single member Florida LLC (See page 169). The revised Florida statute specifically protects multi-member Florida LLCs and explicitly exposes equity in single member Florida LLCs.

Judicial Interpretation

The other side of the coin is how local judges "interpret" the applicable charging order remedy. The cases reveal a general judicial trend toward weakening the charging order creditor limitation. A Maryland court, for example, confirmed the UPA foreclosure rights in *Lauer Construction*.[227] The court ruled that the UPA enforcement mechanism authorized foreclosure of a general partner's interest in profits and surplus of the partnership.[228] The court noted that, in choosing a

---

[227] *Lauer Constr. V. Schrift*, 716 A. 2d 1096 (Md. App. 1998).
[228] *Id.* at 1099.

jurisdiction, the judicial "interpretation" of the applicable statute should be carefully studied. This illustrates the importance of analyzing the cases defining the applicable statute prior to choosing a particular partnership or LLC.

At least one state court has complied with the protective RULPA provision adopted by North Carolina. In *Herring v. Keasler*, the Court of Appeals prevented a creditor from seizing and selling the debtor's North Carolina LLC interest. The original creditor, Branch Banking & Trust Company, obtained a judgment against Bennett Keasler, for nearly $30,000. BB&T assigned the judgment to Max Herring who, in turn, attempted to collect on the judgment by seizing Mr. Keasler's interests in several LLCs. The trial court refused to liquidate Mr. Keasler's LLC interests. Affirming the trial court's decision, the appeals court prohibited transfer of membership interests to Mr. Herring, unless the LLC's operating agreement so authorized.[229]

In the case of *In re Stocks*, the Bankruptcy Court confirmed that Florida's Limited Partnership Act (based on RULPA) limits creditors to a charging order.[230] The Court distinguished the limited partnership charging order from UPA (regarding general partnerships), holding that the latter permits foreclosure of a partner's interest while the former does not contain such a remedy.[231] Several other courts in Virginia and New Hampshire have

---

[229] *Herring v. Keasler*, 563 S.E. 2d 614, 615, 620 (N.C. App. 2002).

[230] *In re Stocks*, 110 B.R. 65 (Bankr. N.D. Fla. 1989).

[231] *Id.* at 66-7.

similarly ruled (or suggested) that the 1976 RULPA format prohibits foreclosure of a debtor's equity interest.

In a contrasting ruling, a Georgia court authorized foreclosure of a 1976 RULPA partnership interest. However, Georgia's statutory language was amended in 2009 to generally prohibit foreclosure.[232]

One Ohio case reflects the propensity of some courts to simply ignore charging order protection. In *Banc One Capital Partners v. Russell*,[233] the Ohio court actually allowed a creditor with a charging order to exercise an option owned by the LLC. The Ohio court held that the creditor (with a 1976 RULPA style charging order) was a "member" of the LLC and, as such, could exercise the option held by the entity (without any managerial authority or voting interest).[234] The ruling is apparently without legal merit but reveals the constant presence of unpredictable judicial "legislation" and the importance of choosing a protective state statute with supportive case law.

Under certain circumstances, a creditor of a limited partner may attempt to circumvent the charging order limitation by arguing that the limited partnership lacks a business purpose. In such case (the argument goes) the limited partnership should be disregarded as a separate

---

[232] Official Code of Georgia Annotated O.C.G.A. § 14-11-504 (Ga. L. 2009, p. 108, § 7/HB 308).

[233] *Banc One Capital Partners v. Russell*, 1999 WL 435787 (Ohio App. 8 Dist. 1999).

[234] *Id.* at 4-5.

entity (exposing its assets to the creditor of a debtor/partner). The creditor could then attach the limited partnership's assets directly.

In *Evans v. Galardi* (1976), the two individual limited partners also owned the corporate general partner. The creditor (of the owners) argued that, since the debtors were each entitled to one-half of partnership profits, they together owned all interest in (exposed) partnership assets. The California Supreme Court held that a limited partner owns no exposed interest in partnership assets. Therefore, a creditor of a partner cannot reach partnership assets. The Court also confirmed that charging orders have "replaced levies of execution as the remedy for reaching such interests." Interestingly, the Court limited its holding by stating, that "[w]here... the partnership is a viable business organization... there is no reason to permit deviation from the prescribed statutory process."[235] The suggestion is that, when a limited partnership is not a "viable business organization," the court may rule that the charging order is not the exclusive remedy.

In 1989, a California Appeals Court actually allowed the sale of a limited partnership interest to satisfy a judgment creditor.[236] Although the non-debtor partners consented to the sale, the Court made clear that, as long as the statute did not absolutely bar the sale of the partnership interest, judicial sale of a charged interest is permissible.[237]

---

[235] *Evans v. Galardi,* 546 P. 2d 313, 320-3 (Cal. 1976).

[236] *Crocker Nat. Bank v. Perroton*, 208 Cal. App. 3d 1, 255 Cal. Rptr. 794 (Cal. App. 1 Dist. 1989).

[237] *Id.*

Correspondingly, in 1991, another California Appeals Court held that a limited partnership interest (under ULPA) may be foreclosed as long as doing so does not unduly interfere with the "business" of the limited partnership.[238]

In 1991, the Delaware legislature eliminated the "viable business" requirement for its LLCs. To avoid judicial intervention, Delaware clarified its LLC statute to state that "[a] limited liability company may carry on any lawful business, purpose or activity, whether or not for profit."[239] In light of the amendment, Delaware is likely the most protective LLC jurisdiction for passive investment.

Taxable Income

Florida, Alabama and Kentucky have arguably broadened the scope of the charging order concept by attributing charging lien owners with taxable profits and losses. These states potentially saddle the creditor with taxable allocations of partnership or LLC income, gain, loss, deduction, credit, and similar items (otherwise attributable to the debtor/owner).[240] Such statutory language could, if endorsed by the courts, encumber creditors with any tax liability attributable to the interest charged (even if no distributions are made). The creditor would be treated as an assignee, and issued an IRS Form

---

[238] *Hellman v. Anderson*, 233 Cal. App. 3d 840, 845-47, (Cal. Ct. App. 3 Dist. 1991).

[239] De. Code Ann. § 18-106(a).

[240] Fl. Stat. § 620.152(1)(c)(1999).

K-1 (reflecting its allocable partnership/LLC taxable income). As a result, the creditor could become responsible for tax on undistributed profits. The applicable partnership/operating agreement may bolster the likelihood of tax attribution to the creditor by requiring the entity to issue the K-1 to the holder of a charging order.[241] The IRS has not, however, taken a definitive position on whether charging order creditors are liable for tax on partnership/LLC profits.

Series LLCs

Assets held in a single business entity are exposed to all creditors of the entity. For example, a professional practice or operating business may incur ordinary obligations for employee compensation and office supplies. The same business could also be hit with a large workers' compensation or tort liability claim. Such an "extraordinary" claim is often not fully insured and may expose the business to insolvency. Proper planning will limit a business' exposure to such extraordinary claims.

Prudent investors and business owners often segregate valuable business and investment assets from assets which attract liability. For example, the segregation of various parcels of real estate (into separate business entities) insulates each parcel from claims associated with the other properties. A similar strategy is to limit the holdings of an active business to only those assets

---

[241] Banc One Capital Partners v. Russell, 1999 WL 435787 (Ohio Ct. App. 8 Dist. 1999).

absolutely required to be held within the operating entity (exposed to business liabilities).

The use of multiple entities to segregate real estate and other assets from business and investment liabilities can, however, be cumbersome. The expense associated with reorganizing an existing business or an investment company into a conglomerate (separating various business and real estate assets among different entities) may also be considerable and potentially complex from a tax perspective.

In an attempt to more efficiently address the issue of liability segregation, several states (Delaware, Illinois, Iowa, Nevada, Oklahoma, Tennessee, Texas, and Utah) have enacted legislation to establish the "series" LLC. Puerto Rico also offers a series LLC. The series LLC may operate through several individual "series." The debts and liabilities associated with one series are collectable only against the assets held by that particular series. The owners of the series LLC may operate independent businesses (or hold several properties) within a single LLC, while statutorily segregating (in different series) the assets and liabilities of each business (or property). The series LLC avoids the costs associated with organizing and maintaining a conglomerate of entities. New series (additional independent units) may be added and existing series may be deleted by simply amending the LLC organizational documents.

There are very specific organizational requirements which must be satisfied to properly organize a series LLC.

Also, although the series LLC offers administrative simplicity and cost savings, the statutory protections have not been tested by the courts (either in the home state or in any state not offering the series LLC). Moreover, the IRS has not issued final guidance regarding the tax status of each series. Proposed regulations suggest that each series will be treated as a separate entity for tax purposes.[242] The tax issues become especially complex if multiple parties own different interests in the various series.

Foreign LLCs

A few foreign countries have adopted limited liability company statutes. Such laws include enhanced charging order protection and onerous procedural obstacles to collection. Foreign LLC statutes may also include very limited statutory periods of limitation to reverse a fraudulent transfer. The most popular debtor friendly nations derive significant revenue from trust, LLC and international business company filings by foreigners seeking the most protective laws. Courts in debtor friendly jurisdictions therefore tend to favor the foreign debtor, to attract the filing fees, registered agent fees, etc. associated with continued use of the jurisdiction for LLCs and trusts. Courts in such jurisdictions have historically upheld LLC protections to avoid creating precedent leading to any loss of government revenue.[243]

---

[242] Treas. Reg. § 301-7701-1(a).

[243] Jay D. Adkisson and Christopher M. Riser, *Asset Protection: Concepts & Strategies for Protecting Your Wealth*, 72-74 McGraw-Hill Publishing, New York (2004).

St. Christopher and Nevis is a federated nation of two small islands in the Caribbean which gained independence from the British Crown in 1983. The federation's constitution empowers the island of Nevis to independently legislate certain trust and corporate law. Nevis arguably offers the most protective offshore LLC.[244] In light of the rejection of single member LLC protections by several U.S. courts, the single member Nevis LLC (funded abroad) may be a solo LLC alternative. If properly formed, the Nevis LLC may also be disregarded for U.S. tax purposes. Also, the names of members and managers of Nevis LLCs are not public information.

In addition to charging order protection and the advantages intrinsic to offshore entities, proposed revisions to the Nevis LLC Act (to which the author is contributing) will further limit creditors. Such proposed amendments include the following:

- Nevis will not recognize foreign judgments or conflicting laws regarding charging order claims.[245]

- Any creditor challenging the funding of a Nevis LLC must hire a Nevis attorney to handle the matter.

---

[244] The Nevis Limited Liability Company Ordinance of 1995, Amended January 1, 2002.

[245] *See* The Cook Islands Limited Liability Companies Act of 2008 § 45, enacting similar language.

- The Nevis attorney is prohibited from taking the case on contingency (forcing the creditor to come out of pocket to file suit).

- The manager must ignore distribution requests coerced by a foreign court if a duress clause is included in the LLC's Operating Agreement.

- Fraudulent transfer claims regarding the funding of a Nevis LLC are prohibited if LLC equity represents fair value received by the debtor.

- Proof beyond a reasonable doubt is required to prove fraudulent transfers to a Nevis LLC.

- Proof of the debtor's insolvency is required for any fraudulent transfer claim.

- The creditor may not prove fraudulent transfer "constructively" but must always prove fraudulent intent.

- Shortened statute of limitations apply to any claim of fraudulent transfer to a Nevis LLC.

- The debtor member and LLC may recover from an unsuccessful plaintiff all costs and fees of litigation.

- The creditor must post a bond before filing suit, to secure payment of all litigation costs of the debtor member, in the event the creditor loses his collection suit.

Thus, under the proposed statute, if a member of a Nevis LLC becomes subject to a U.S. judgment, the creditor must apply Nevis law to reach LLC assets. The creditor must post bond and prove his case again in Nevis because Nevis will not allow for enforcement of U.S. judgments. The costs associated with bringing suit in Nevis are astronomical and may not be shifted to a Nevis attorney working on contingency. Aside from government claims involving a quickly detected fraudulent transfer, collection from a Nevis LLC is typically an exercise in frustration. The proposed changes, if adopted, will further discourage creditors.

As discussed at Section 6.2, the risk associated with using offshore entities is that a U.S. court accepting jurisdiction may be tempted to ignore applicable foreign law. If the defendant is sufficiently unsavory, U.S. courts will typically favor a judgment creditor, to preserve the effectiveness of the U.S. litigation system.

A creditor may move to set aside (i.e. disregard) LLC protections by arguing that the LLC is nothing more than a sham controlled by the founder or an "alter ego" of the debtor with no business purpose. If the owner of an entity fails to treat the company as a separate legal person, then his creditors may likewise ignore any outside LLC protections and reach LLC assets. If successful, the creditor is not limited to a charging order, but may access the underlying assets of the entity itself.[246]

To limit such exposure to reverse veil piercing (i.e., loss of LLC equity to a personal creditor), assets held by an offshore LLC should remain outside the jurisdiction of U.S. courts. The most protective foreign LLC is (i) managed by a non-U.S. resident individual or a company with no ties to the U.S. and (ii) funded with foreign assets.

As discussed in Section 6.2, if a debtor refuses to return foreign LLC assets to the U.S. (for collection), a U.S. judgment may be enforced through judicial threat of incarceration. Such cases have, however, enjoyed limited success. The line of cases suggests that incarceration for contempt is a concern only in cases involving disgraceful debtor behavior, reactionary transfers and/or the breach of federal bankruptcy or commercial regulations.

The absence of lawsuits challenging LLCs governed by foreign law suggests that collection disputes are typically settled in favor of the debtor. Provided that the debtor funded the offshore structure prior to any present (or reasonably expected) creditor claim, offshore LLC planning should thwart even the most aggressive creditor. The courts all chant the same warning: Plan for a rainy day. Once the clouds start to form, it's too late to seek shelter.

---

[246] *See, e.g., In re Turner*, 335 B.R. 140 (Bankr. N.D. Cal. 2005), modified 345 B.R. 674 (N.D. Cal. 2006).

Asset Protection

Chapter 8: A Word on Confidentiality

"Fraud and deceit abound in these days more than in former times" - Sir Edward Coke (1602)[247]

A truly well considered asset protection plan is not based on confidentiality and should be transparent in litigation. A U.S. debtor's assets and other financial information are always discoverable through domestic litigation. Unless the debtor flees the U.S. or lies at deposition (potentially triggering a variety of repercussions), all information associated with the debtor's assets may be discovered. U.S. judges are typically infuriated by the hiding of assets and are much more

---

[247] Sir Edward Coke, *Twyne's Case*, 3. Co. 80 (1602).

amenable to a forthright debtor (relying on legitimate planning).

Although confidentiality of financial information may facilitate asset protection (because the creditor must first identify and locate available assets), the concept of confidentiality should not be confused with legal creditor protections. Asset protection is not a means of hiding assets; it is a strategy to legally place assets beyond the reach of future unanticipated and unknown creditors.

A related misconception regarding asset protection involves tax evasion. The secrecy available in several debtor havens has historically created a temptation among certain misinformed Americans to hide taxable income. Such tax evasion is illegal and actively policed by the IRS.

Several debtor havens have enacted secrecy laws to protect the confidentiality of foreign investment. Such disclosure restrictions may not, however, apply if the creditor is the IRS. The U.S. is now a party to eighty-five tax treaties which reduce double taxation between the treaty partners.[248] All but one of such treaties contain "exchange of information" provisions, to prevent tax fraud in the treaty countries. The language varies from treaty to

---

[248] Internal Revenue Service ("IRS") Department of the Treasury, IRS Publication 901 "U.S. Tax Treaties" (April 2011) *available at* http://www.irs.gov/pub/irs-pdf/p901.pdf, *see also* Worksheet 2: Status of U.S. Tax Treaties and International Tax Agreements, Bloomberg BNA, January 13, 2009, *available at* http://taxandaccounting.bna.com/btac/display/batch_print_display. adp?searchid=16449429.

treaty but generally requires treaty partners to disclose information relevant to enforcement of the tax laws of each party. Such information may include otherwise confidential banking and financial records.

The IRS routinely exchanges financial information with its tax treaty partners. Such information typically involves passive income and bank account deposits by Americans in the foreign country. For example, regular bank deposits by a U.S. resident in a treaty country will likely be disclosed by the foreign treaty partner and processed by the IRS Service Center in Bensalem, Pennsylvania.

In addition, over the last twenty years, the IRS has pursued foreign tax information from governments which have not signed a U.S. tax treaty. To obtain financial information from non-treaty partners, the IRS negotiates tax information exchange agreements ("TIEAs"). For example, the IRS has focused on establishing TIEAs in the Caribbean, given the substantial U.S. investment and business activities in the region and the general absence of tax treaties. The U.S. has entered into tax treaties with Barbados, Bermuda, Jamaica and Trinidad and Tobago. The U.S. signed TIEAs with Antigua and Barbuda, Bahamas, Cayman Islands, British Virgin Islands and Netherlands Antilles.[249]

---

[249] *See* Global Forum on Transparency and Exchange of Information for Tax Purposes, "Exchange of Tax Information Agreements." A complete list of TIEAs (worldwide) *available at* http://www.oecd.org/document/3/0,3746,en_21571361_43854757_48561219_1_1_1_1,00.html.

The TIEA information exchange provisions are similar to the analogous treaty language. The agreements allow for the exchange of financial information associated with the collection of tax. The benefits offered by the U.S. to potential TIEA partners include U.S. tax deductions for business meetings and seminars in participating countries and tax favorable loans. Also, a potential TIEA partner may be attracted to the arrangement because it provides access to U.S. tax information on its own citizens.

The U.S. also participates in a Mutual Collection Assistance Program (MCAP) with five countries: Canada, France, Denmark, Sweden and the Netherlands.[250] Each of the parties assists the others in the collection of taxes. Under MCAP, the "requested" country will actually collect taxes owed by a citizen of the "requesting" country (residing in the requested country). Personal information, such as the individual's name, address, identification number, type of tax, amount of tax, and any other necessary information is exchanged between the countries.

Treaties, TIEAs, and the MCAP program expand IRS access to the identity and location of all U.S. taxpayer

---

[250] 11.3.25; Disclosure to Foreign Countries to Tax Treatment: Disclosures to Foreign countries in Collection Matters, Internal Revenue Manual, June 19, 2009, *available at* http://www.irs.gov/irm/part11/irm_11-003-025.html; *see also* Michael Sullivan, IRS Mutual Collection Assistance Program-Canada, Denmark, France, Netherlands, February 11, 2011, *available at* http://www.freshstarttax.com/blog/irs-mutual-collection-assistance-program-canada, last accessed January 29, 2012.

assets. The U.S. investor abroad should take particular care to avoid turning the IRS into a creditor.

Chapter 9: Property and Casualty Insurance

"Never lend your car to anyone to whom you have given birth." – Erma Bombeck

9.1   General and Professional Liability

Asset protection planning does not replace the need for insurance.   A prudent asset protection plan includes both individual and business liability coverage. Liability insurance (as opposed to property coverage) contractually obligates an insurer to pay for unintentional damages caused by the insured to other people and property.   Liability coverage creates a contractual right to reimbursement (for liabilities otherwise exposing the insured).   Property insurance protects the insured's physical assets from damage by other people, accidents and natural disasters. Both property and liability insurance are necessary, but liability insurance is typically more relevant in asset protection planning.

Liability insurance reduces exposure to (i) personal claims (such as auto liability or injury to a house guest), (ii) general business liabilities and (iii) professional malpractice claims. Adequate personal and professional coverage creates an initial barrier against the loss of unprotected assets.

Individuals with significant assets should carry homeowners' and auto liability insurance (including "uninsured motorist" coverage), as well as an "umbrella" policy (extending such coverage) for several million dollars. Exclusions from personal liability coverage, for damages arising from business activity, dangerous sports, power tools and dog bites, to name a few, should be carefully studied.

Business claims (associated with damages arising from the operation of a company) generally expose only assets of the particular business. Assets held separately are not exposed to claims related to the operation of the business entity. As discussed in Chapter 7, corporations and LLCs provide "inside" asset protection by insulating owners from corporate obligations. Business assets are exposed to business vendors or client claims (arising "inside" that specific business operation). Business liability insurance protects the value of property owned by the company.

General business insurance covers liability from accidents on the business premises and otherwise arising from an employee acting within the scope of employment. Typically excluded from coverage are harm caused by intentional acts of employees, acts while intoxicated, discrimination, business activities at home, board and officer decisions and contractual obligations. Limited specialty coverage is available for certain exclusions, namely, discrimination, sexual harassment, business activities at home and board of directors liability.

Professionals, such as doctors, lawyers, engineers, and architects are personally liable for professional negligence. They may also be liable for the acts of employees. Although technically a business liability, responsibility for professional negligence is also a personal obligation of the professional. Given the insurance coverage traditionally available to doctors, lawyers, engineers and other professionals, U.S. tort law governing professional negligence has developed around the availability of malpractice insurance. Plaintiffs' attorneys specializing in professional negligence tend to seek recovery from an insurance carrier. This allows the plaintiff's attorney to focus on the validity of the claim (without concern regarding collection of the eventual judgment). Common exclusions from malpractice coverage (leaving the professional exposed) are damages from gross negligence, punitive damages, acts of uninsured subordinate employees and defective products.

Business and professional liability coverage typically represent a greater expense than personal coverage. Cost is a substantial factor in deciding how much business and professional negligence coverage to carry.

Businesses should also consider employee harassment and related coverage, to "contract away" as much employee liability as possible. All businesses should establish an employee handbook, to define the parameters of acceptable conduct. The handbook should mandate general policies, to shield against frivolous employee claims.

Contractual restrictions on competition and disclosure of confidential business information should be required of employees, as a condition to new and continued employment. Reasonable non-disclosure provisions are enforceable. The scope of permissible restrictions on competition, varies from state to state. Employment agreements should also burden the losing party (in litigation involving the agreement) with the legal fees incurred by the winner. The risk of having to pay both lawyers will often deter an employee contemplating a breach. Without such language, the parties usually pay their own legal fees.

Although certain imprudent advisors take the position that minimal or no insurance will make for a less attractive defendant, a reasonable and affordable level of coverage, combined with a carefully developed asset protection plan, is the most effective approach. Insurance coverage will often pacify an aggressive plaintiff's attorney with "low-hanging fruit," while a sound asset protection plan will protect the "tree" from attack. Most plaintiffs' attorneys work for a fee contingent on collection (not on an hourly basis). If damages are not recovered, the attorney is not paid for his or her time and must cover all costs of litigating the claim. Immediately available insurance proceeds typically satiate a trial lawyer, otherwise forced to analyze and attack the weaknesses of the debtor's asset protection plan. Even large professional claims are often settled for a reasonable amount of insurance.

9.2   Auto Liability

An often overlooked area of liability exposure stems from the use of automobiles by someone other than the owner. Depending on the applicable state, the owner of a car may be responsible for its operation by another person. Such laws can be unpredictable and contribute to the most common source of personal liability in the United States. The attribution of auto liability from one person to another is based on the "strict liability" of the owner for operation of the car. Auto liability planning is crucial to avoid strict owner liability.

In Florida, for example, an individual owner of a vehicle is strictly liable for its operation by anyone borrowing the car. Strict liability does not depend on actual negligence or intent to do harm, but a strict duty to make something safe. By lending a car to a friend in Florida, the owner becomes liable for any damages caused by the friend.[251] The different state statutes include an array of limitations and variations on the scope of strict auto liability. For example, in California, an automobile owner is strictly liable for accidents occurring from any driver's use of the automobile. The owner's liability, however, is limited to $5,000 of property damage, $15,000 for death or injury to a single person, and $30,000 for death or injury to multiple parties.[252]

Florida further attributes liability to the car owner through a doctrine known as negligent entrustment of a dangerous instrumentality. If (i) a vehicle owner knew or should have known that the borrower was not competent or prepared to drive, (ii) the entrustment of the vehicle created an appreciable risk of harm to others and (iii) the harm was caused by the negligence of the entruster, the plaintiff may prove a case for negligent entrustment.

A notable source of auto liability attribution is from children (potentially even adult children). In several states, both parents are liable for the operation of a vehicle by a minor child. Children of any age operating a car at an adult's direction (such as a request to run errands) may expose the adult to the negligence of the driver. The attribution of child liability to the parent can create what is known as a "gap in coverage." The gap occurs because children are often uninsured (or under insured). Such inadequate coverage of the child may not satisfy damages

---

[251] Fl. Stat. § 324.021(9((b)(3) (2009).
[252] Ca. Vehicle Code § 17151(a) (2011).

(for which the child and parents are liable) and the parent's policy does not cover the negligence of the child.

Although more expensive, prudence often dictates adding the child (of any age) living at home to a family policy with high coverage limits. The family policy will also (typically) cover the use of rental cars. Several types of policies are available nationally which cover the head of household, spouse and children. In addition, umbrella liability coverage (to augment auto and homeowners' coverage) is generally available, starting from coverage of one million dollars. An umbrella policy may be underwritten to cover boats, RVs and other vehicles. Such coverage can be a very affordable way to practically eliminate exposure to home, auto and related claims.

Companies are not liable for the driving accidents of employees not "on the job." The employer may, however, cover an employee and his family for personal use of a company car if identified as a "permissive operator" in the company policy. Commercial auto insurance typically includes such coverage and insures employees driving a company car (on the job or otherwise). Such coverage is limited to use of the company car unless the policy includes an endorsement (called "Drive Other Car Coverage") insuring accidents by the employee (and family) driving other cars.

The company should also insure against any liability caused by an employee driving his or her own car on company business. This coverage is called "Employers Non-Owned Auto Liability."

Individual drivers without commercial coverage should be aware of the fact that insurers often deny coverage (under a personal policy) for accidents related to incidental business use of a car. Examples of incidental business use include picking up a business document or visiting a rental property.

9.3   Conclusion

Insurance planning requires astute lifestyle and contractual risk shifting. Shifting liability to the insurer (to the extent economically feasible) is always advisable. Unfortunately, most Americans are underinsured because they have an unreasonably low tolerance for insurance premiums. The lack of adequate insurance coverage shifts liability exposure to wealthier defendants (who have the assets to pay the judgment). Potential defendants with assets to protect should maintain coverage sufficient to anticipate any reasonable contingency.

Chapter 10: Equity Stripping

"Lend money to an enemy, and thou will gain him, to a friend and then will lose him." – Benjamin Franklin

Despite the availability of asset protection techniques, some assets cannot be practically transferred or liquidated. Obstacles include tax issues, unavailable partner consents and title encumbrances. Integration of such assets into a protective structure or conversion to creditor exempt assets is therefore not feasible.

A simple strategy known as "equity stripping" may be implemented to protect non-transferrable exposed property. The technique involves depleting the property of value. The property owner borrows money, the repayment of which is secured by the lender's lien on the property. The lender must have an enforceable right to foreclose the secured property if the loan is not timely paid. Once the lien is recorded, the property may not be reached by a later judgment creditor without first paying the secured loan. The borrowed money is then invested in a protected asset (such as whole life insurance, an annuity or the owner's homestead) or used to purchase assets in a protected structure.

Equity stripping (i) protects otherwise exposed property value and (ii) allows for the productive investment of otherwise stagnant equity. Care must be taken, however, to ensure the preservation of sufficient liquidity. Despite the benefits of equity stripping, protections which compromise the borrower's ability to make payments on the loan should be avoided. Sufficient cash reserves should always be available to support the debt and the cost of litigation.

Some advisors recommend unrestricted borrowing from a "friendly" lender (such as a wealthy friend or relative), with no intention of enforcing repayment. Such arrangements are highly scrutinized by the courts. Familial loans made in good faith may, however, be utilized to encumber unprotected property. Having a parent lien property of a child borrower will force the child's creditor to pay the parents before reaching the secured assets. Familial loans should be properly evidenced by a promissory note (reflecting the date of the loan) and applicable lien filing. Such loans provide a means of paying mom and dad (with unprotected assets), as an alternative to paying a judgment creditor. The more carefully documented the related party loan, the lower the risk of a judge disregarding the loan, "stripping" the lien and attaching the collateral.

Another way to achieve equity stripping is through the segregation of business assets. For example, commercial real estate occupied by an active business may be separately acquired by an LLC (formed by the business owners) and leased to the business entity. This strategy segregates the property from business creditors and keeps employees away from valuable real estate and equipment.

The real estate LLC (which leases commercial space to the business entity) may establish (i) an onerous landlord lien (encumbering business assets to secure lease payments) and (ii) lease acceleration rights (causing all lease payments to become due upon the business entering litigation). The lease can establish landlord liens on all business property, including accounts receivable, machinery and contract rights. In the event that the business entity enters litigation or suffers a judgment, a huge lease acceleration obligation encumbers all business assets. The landlord can foreclose its lien, with attachment priority superior to the business creditor. The landlord lien forces a judgment creditor to pay the entire lease before reaching any business assets.

Another equity stripping strategy is to allow a real estate lender to lien unprotected assets of the business (as collateral for its loan). This prevents creditors of the business from reaching business assets encumbered by the lender.

Accounts receivable ("A/R") can also be converted to cash by selling the A/R to a "factor." A factor is in the business of purchasing A/R at a discount. Factoring allows for immediate cash flow and the distribution of exposed cash from the business. Alternatively, the business can borrow against A/R and invest the loan proceeds in protected assets. The lender records a lien against the A/R, to equity strip its value. Once the Uniform Commercial Code lien is filed, any creditor of the business must pay the loan before reaching A/R. Several commercial insurers actually arrange financed A/R programs as a means of funding owner retirement plans with insurance and annuities.

Any factoring structure or loan by a related party should include a market factoring premium (for a factored sale) or market interest rate. The choice between an A/R sale or a loan (secured by A/R), will often depend on the tax impact of each option. If related parties own both the business and lender (or factor), they must carefully maintain corporate formalities and meticulously document the arrangement.

Final Chapter: Case Study

This Chapter illustrates how to apply some of the most common tax neutral asset protection techniques. In our hypothetical example, Jack and Jill are a married couple with children, living in Anytown, USA. Jill is a radiologist, who loves real estate investment. She owns the radiology practice with an equal partner, through a professional "S" corporation. In addition to the radiology practice, the "S" corporation owns "free and clear" a professional building (where the medical practice operates). The medical practice itself holds no other significant assets, apart from accounts receivable. Jill has no written agreement with her partner regarding the ownership or management of the practice.

Jill individually owns four rental houses. She also holds several personal savings and securities accounts which build value while she searches for her next investment property. Jill contributes to a 401(k) retirement plan through the radiology practice.

Jack owns and operates a paving construction company through an "S" corporation. Jack has a young minority partner to whom he intends to one day sell the business. The paving business operates in leased space, but owns substantial heavy equipment. The business generates consistent profit, and has a high market value with little debt. Jack works constantly and reinvests his free cash into the business. Jack has never solidified a succession arrangement with his partner.

Jack and Jill own a home together with substantial equity. They hold no other joint assets.

Jill

Jill's main liability exposure is a potential medical malpractice claim. An adverse judgment against either Jill or her partner exposes the practice assets and the personal assets of the defendant/physician. A judgment against Jill exposes her personal real estate, cash and securities.

Jill and her business partner should first reorganize the medical practice by moving the office building to a protective LLC (formed in a favorable jurisdiction). The reorganization could take a variety of forms, depending on the tax circumstances.

The medical building LLC should be owned 50% by Jill and Jack (TBE) and 50% by Jill's partner and spouse (TBE). TBE titling will (depending on the applicable state law) insulate LLC equity from charging liens, except for joint debts owed by both husband and wife. The transfer of the building will insulate it from any future medical malpractice claims. Inside liability, arising from an accident in the building, would be limited (beyond insurance coverage) to loss of the building (the sole asset of the LLC).

The new landlord LLC could establish a lien on the accounts receivable of the medical practice. The lien (securing rents outstanding) would hinder the attachment of A/R by creditors of the practice. The practice entity and/or the new building LLC could also establish a commercial line of credit, secured by the practice A/R, to equity strip the practice receivables. A sale of the A/R to a factor could also be considered.

Applicable formalities of the professional corporation should be brought up to date. The practice entity should also be converted to a professional LLC, to limit equity claims by any outside creditor (of Jill or her partner). The LLC will require less formality and maintenance than the existing professional corporation. For example, LLCs require no annual minutes.

Both the practice LLC and the medical building LLC should purchase a reasonable amount of malpractice and property and casualty insurance (as applicable).

Insurance proceeds will provide "low hanging fruit" to a potential claimant and offset litigation costs.

To avoid any partner conflicts, the medical building LLC should be governed by an operating agreement linked to the medical practice. If a physician leaves the practice, the agreement would allow (or require) the remaining physician (and spouse) to purchase the membership interest of the exiting physician (and spouse). The agreement could require the purchase of life insurance, to provide liquidity for a buyout triggered by the death of either physician. Correspondingly, the practice entity should be governed by an operating agreement, to make management decisions and any necessary practice transition uneventful.

Jill should contribute the real estate she owns personally, along with a substantial amount of her more liquid assets, to a family LLC (discussed below). Individual ownership of real estate exposes Jill to claims arising from an accident on any property. Moreover, property held individually is available to Jill's creditors.

Jill's 401(k) account is ERISA based and therefore protected from her creditors. Any money withdrawn from the 401(k) likely becomes exposed to creditors, and should be deposited into a subsidiary of the family LLC.

Jack

Jack should consider conversion of his valuable construction corporation to an LLC (taxed as an "S" corporation). The existing corporation offers no "outside" creditor protection. Jack's business equity (and the equity held by Jack's minority partner) is exposed to their respective "outside" creditors. Jack's new LLC interest could also be titled as TBE with Jill (if available in their state) to avoid charging order exposure to Jack's outside creditors.

Any valuable construction equipment should be transferred to a separate LLC, and leased back to the construction LLC. The equipment would typically be transferred to a sister entity (of the construction LLC), depending on the tax consequences. Subsequent to the transfer, employees, suppliers and other business claimants of the construction company would likely have no access to the valuable machinery. Management and ownership of the sister equipment LLC would correspond with the construction LLC, owned by Jack and his younger minority partner. The segregation of equipment in a sister LLC is analogous to Jill's segregation of the medical office in an LLC (which leases space to Jill's medical practice). Jack could also strip equity from the equipment by establishing a line of credit, secured by the equipment.

An operating agreement for the construction company will allow Jack to sell majority ownership to his younger partner (over time), without losing managerial control. If Jack were to die before the sale of his entire interest, the operating agreement could require Jack's partner to purchase Jack's interest with life insurance proceeds (maintained pursuant to the operating agreement). The agreement would also allow Jack to repurchase equity sold to his partner, in the event his partner leaves the business.

Family LLC

Jack and Jill should form a protective LLC or limited partnership holding company. The holding company would own five subsidiary LLCs. Jill's securities accounts would be re-titled in the name of a securities subsidiary and each of her four rental properties would be deeded to a separate subsidiary. The subsidiaries (disregarded for tax purposes) would segregate Jill's securities and each piece of investment real estate. As a result of such segregation, any liability arising from a single property would be insulated from the other properties. Additional subsidiaries would be formed for each additional piece of real estate purchased. Any new securities accounts can be opened by the securities subsidiary (formed in Delaware, to take advantage of Delaware's protective statutory language regarding passive assets). The various securities accounts (unlike real estate) are not individually segregated because none creates inside liability (potentially exposing the other property in the same subsidiary). Note that the holding company would likely elect to be taxed as a partnership which precludes it from owning equity in either Jack's or Jill's business/practice entity (each taxed as an "S" corp).

Thus, the five subsidiary LLCs would segregate Jill's liquid securities and eliminate shared liability between investment properties. Liability exposure arising from a particular property (held in an LLC subsidiary) would be limited to the loss of the property (if damages exceed insurance coverage). Moreover, any unforeseen creditor of Jill or Jack would not be able to reach any assets of the holding company (or of any subsidiary).

Jill and Jack should consider organizing a management (sixth) LLC subsidiary. The management LLC would handle all management, back-office, and administrative functions associated with Jill's real estate and the medical building. Such management subsidiary would eliminate the need for active involvement (and exposure) of the holding company. The management entity would hold management contract rights and all accounting/computer type assets. A management agreement would establish a service arrangement for accounting, rental collection, evictions, repairs, etc. This arrangement would consolidate all check writing, accounting, and collections operations through a single subsidiary.

If Jill is more comfortable with exclusive control, she could act as sole manager of the holding company (owned husband and wife, TBE, if available in their state). If Jill is opposed to involving Jack at all, Jack may be excluded. Excluding Jack, however, eliminates the potential for protective TBE titling of spousal membership interests. Membership interests held by Jill alone are subject to a charging order lien (and, potentially, foreclosure). To avoid exposure as a single member LLC, Jill could form one or more irrevocable trusts to hold minority interests in the holding company. Such trusts would act as additional member(s) and may be controlled by Jill or by a friendly party, for the benefit of Jill's children. An asset protection trust benefitting Jill (and anyone else) could also potentially act as an additional member. The less control and benefit Jill enjoys over any trust/additional member, the less likely a judge will disregard the trust as a second member of the holding company.

An additional layer of protection could be created by contributing the family holding company to a domestic or offshore asset protection trust. Typically, Jill (and/or Jack) would retain managerial control (and 1%) of the LLC. Jill, Jack and/or their kids could be trust beneficiaries. Depending on where the trust is formed, Jill and Jack could retain the right to minimum distributions from the trust.

The use of a holding company structure may also create estate planning opportunities. Jack and Jill can give additional non-controlling interests in the holding company to trusts for their children. Gifts could be made annually to children and grandchildren, or to trusts created for them. An annual program of gifting will reduce their taxable estate and potentially incorporate discounts to the federal gift tax.

Homestead

If Jack and Jill live in a state offering an unlimited homestead exemption, they should retain personal ownership of their home and confirm compliance with the applicable acreage and other conditions. If TBE titling is available, it should be properly established, as an additional protective layer of equity in the home. In states offering a limited homestead exemption, the home should (depending on the circumstances) be moved into the family holding company and/or "stripped" of equity. Jack and Jill should also purchase sufficient homeowner's insurance to guard against liability arising from an accident on the premises. Potential joint liability will expose the house (if not statutorily protected) and all other unprotected assets held individually by either or both spouses. The chart on page 218 illustrates Jack and Jill's protection plan.

Conclusion

By implementing a manageable series of legal protections, Jack and Jill will insulate valuable assets from creditors and prevent business disputes. A properly tailored asset protection plan safeguards wealth. A seasoned attorney dedicated to the practice of asset protection can help you design and implement the best structure for your particular situation.

Asset Protection

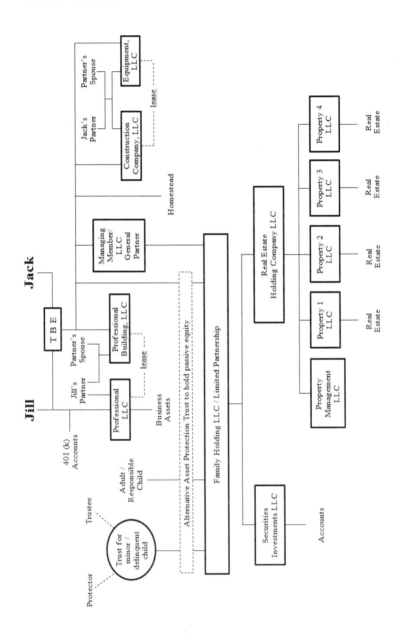

Bibliography

Adkisson, Jay D., and Riser, Christopher M., *Asset Protection: Concepts & Strategies for Protecting Your Wealth*. McGraw-Hill, 2004.

Engel, Barry S., *Asset Protection Planning Guide*. CCH, 2005.

Fisher, Howard, "Domestic Based Asset Protection Strategies Explained and Fantasies Exposed." *Annual Wealth Protection: Hot Topics in Asset Protection Planning* (Florida Bar Seminar), 2006.

Northcott, Alan, *Asset Protection for Business Owners and High Income Earners: How to Protect What You Own from Lawsuits and Creditors*. Atlantic Publishing Group, 2009.

Rosen, Howard D., and Rothschild, Gideon, "Asset Protection Planning." Portfolio No. 810-2d, Tax Management (BNA). *Estates, Gifts and Trusts*, 2007.